PLUCKING THE EAGLE

Bringing Socialism to the United States

A Chronological History of How We Got to Where We Are

by

C. Francis James

INKWATER PRESS

Portland • Oregon
INKWATERPRESS.COM

To:
JGJW
And
T
CRC
P
*Without whose inspiration this book
would not have been written.*

TABLE OF CONTENTS

PLUCKING THE EAGLE

INTRODUCTION

Reading the newspaper or listening to the news about the economy, do you ever wonder about how and why the living and working environment in the United States has eroded from what it used to be; a vibrant exciting prosperous society to what it is today, a downtrodden society with diminishing promise? Concerning the economy, does the thought that the Federal Reserve should not let the recent financial meltdown of the economy from ever happening ever cross your mind? Did you ever wonder how the federal debt appeared, why is it getting worse? Why did taxation happen, why do we have all these forms of taxes and why do they keep going up? Do you ever wonder about the trade barriers, treaties, pacts, deficits and how it affects your wages, jobs strength of the dollar and general welfare? Do you wonder why Health Care costs so much and think of ways the health care industry can cut costs...if only the politicians listened to me you think!! After reading the exasperating news about the Federal Reserve's policies, rate increases, taxes, trade deficits and affordable health care, do you often find yourself saying it "used to be better back in the old days?" Are we, the United States, becoming a "Nanny" state, where more burden is being placed on workers in the form of taxes to care for the increasing number of people dependent on the government for subsistence? If you do, read this book about the how we got to where we are! This book will provide an historical perspective as to the origination of these government run operations and how their true intent is being abused to foster Socialism in America!

PREAMBLE

Socialism- any of various economic and political theories advocating collective or governmental ownership and administration of the means of production and the distribution of goods.

If one were to socialize the world, how would one go about it? Would one do it alone? Impossible! One would need a group. When a group becomes established, what means and actions does this group use to accomplish its socialistic goals? Where does this group get its origin and how does it perpetuate itself? How does one get invited into this group? Once invited in, how does one expand this group to where it can actually change the world? How would a group of individuals together form some sort of means to socialize the world; to create a world void of individual nations? How would they create a world where the masses are subjected to the machinations of the few? How would this group gain control of all nations? How would this group eliminate boundaries, dismantle sovereign nations, control the economies, subjugate the citizens to their wishes and forge many small independent nations into a mass of hemispheric entities? How would this group take this world made up of 250 nations, and through their diabolical and disastrous international economic schemes and political policies, reshape the sovereignty of nations into a socialistic world where many will be ruled by the few?

Many people have seen this happening for a hundred

or so years. Most have not. It is my intention to show how this sinister group is socializing the world where we as private citizens, who make our own decisions, manage our own money, elect our own officials to run our government, are losing control to the point of us becoming subjects of the imperial few. I intend to illustrate how these individuals have banded together into a group I will refer to as "Globalists" who have used their influence in their respective careers, be it politics, business, or industry and have manipulated events in their favor to achieve their ultimate goal of one world socialism. Part of their objective is to accumulate for themselves into the hands of the few, the world's wealth and natural resources to perpetuate their goals and to achieve their desired result; a one world socialistic government.

Socialism is defined by Webster as: "Any and various economic and political theories advocating collective or governmental ownership and administration of the means of production and distribution of goods." If you don't think this is happening today and has been happening for years, in what beach is your head buried? Try to buy a car, or a house, pay your taxes, wonder about the trade and federal deficits, the actions of the Federal Reserve, its effect on the dollar, economy and its' impact on workers, and figure out the right health care for your family without some sort of government intervention. With diminishing disposable income to buy homes, cars, and health care, and increasing taxes, how has the government controlled your financial means through misleading economic theories? Why has government spending required the need to increase tax rates on existing taxes, and to originate new taxes on new items?

Of the many methods this group is applying to socialize this country and the world, the four on which I want to concentrate are the Federal Reserve, Trade, Taxes, and Health Care. Why? For two reasons: Because these four sectors have had the most impact financially on the US and the world, and because these four subjects represent the four stages along a work in progress time line in which each are located.

In order for the Globalists to achieve their goal of creating a socialist world, they have to dismantle the financial, economic, cultural and social boundaries of individual nations and rebuild them back up into a collective one world cohesive body politic. It means individuals in each nation will have to surrender former lifestyles and accept the Globalists' devised bigger and overall "improved" method of a socialistic government.

The first of four stages and the preferred method consistent throughout these four sectors that are used to dismantle the aforementioned boundaries is to introduce some form of chaos in the respective sector that will necessitate the creation of an organization, an organization designed by the Globalists, and operated by them for the benefit of their ideals. The second stage is to convene a meeting of these so-called "experts" to devise their remedy. The third step is to allow the "experts" to introduce their socialistic solution to the public. Accompanying the introduction, positive reinforcement of their plan to lend some credence to it is implemented. The fourth stage and completion of the plan is to perpetuate the system by creating organizations out of which come these experts that maintain their plan, manage continued progress towards their goal while simultaneously keeping their ploy hidden from public.

The Federal Reserve came into being in 1913, so entrenched in the minds of public acceptance that removal or revision of operations seems impossible. To the Globalists, controlling the money supply was the surest method of controlling the economy, and because of its impact on the economy, the most reliable way of garnering control over the citizens. Directing citizens to accept the idea of a Central Bank in the form of the Federal Reserve was the second goal. Once accomplished, this allowed the Globalist to lead the citizens on a socialist path accepting the direction they, the Globalists, devised. By manipulating domestic economic activity, Globalists could introduce their socialistic remedies. With the ability to direct business activity in a certain country, they could influence government leaders to follow along. With the leaders of each country compliant, Globalist's monetary system would remain unchallenged as it continued strengthening as each country capitulated to the Globalists ideals of socialistic objectives. A foreign leader desperate for money or economic prosperity will accept the "Conditions" of the loan Globalists make. These are surely agreements to accept the Globalists influence and direction for socialist goals. Once the money supply is controlled, socialistic means can be introduced into other areas of society. In this book, I will offer a brief history outlining the organizations and people who devised this one world agenda, describe the history of money in the US and the birth of the Federal Reserve Board, how it operates, manipulates the financial markets positively or negatively to suit its plan and reveal the secret agenda how the plotters who formed this "cartel" plan to control the economies of every nation on earth.

Trade and taxes are intricately intertwined beginning the trend towards socialism in 1913. In actuality, the income tax was part of the Federal Reserve Act of 1913, so the Globalist passed legislation providing simultaneously for: 1) The Federal Reserve to control and spend the money supply they create, and 2) The means to pay, (Income Tax) for the expenditures!! Through ongoing trade wars and dismantling of sovereign nations through free trade measures, the trade issue is in the work-in-progress mode. Returning to trade policies which enabled previous generations to enjoy the prosperous lifestyles of the 1890's and 1920's is unlikely, possible but unlikely. For one, the protective tariffs that provided for the nascent industrial base to flourish allowing for increased employment generating financial wealth for the public to afford the amenities of the times; the lavish lifestyles of the "Roaring 20's" and with the advent of automobiles and ocean liners, travel and expansion, are considered by many as implausible; implausible to the Globalists who do not want the public to know how well protectionism worked. However, with recent economic events protective measures and discussions are resurfacing. A decision to revive protective measures will remain with the reader after reading the credibility of them in Trade.

Fostering socialism through progressive taxes thereby redistributing wealth also began in 1913. The continuing confiscation of wealth through higher and more taxes stymies production and increases societal dependency on the government, in other words, the advent of a nanny state or socialism! The tax system is flawed. An additional means of generating government revenues, besides over taxation, is needed and while this subject is in the work-in-progress mode as well, debate and restructuring tax policy is constantly in debate. See the definition of socialism. To overhaul the tax system, one needs the assistance of new trade policies and a new business attitude.

The Health Care system and the ongoing debate began after World War II is beyond the nascent stage. If the public blindly accepts the Government's recommendations without information and warnings to the potential outcomes, then the true objective could develop into socialized medicine. In the fifty plus years when health care cost showed up on the radar screen as a hot topic, the public has witnessed and experienced first hand the speed of governmental interference and eventual control of the vast accumulation of expenditures for the health care crisis.

From time to time, relevant and smaller examples found in Connecticut to illustrate the broader but similar problems facing the nation will be used.

HISTORY OF EUROPEAN BANKING/ THE BIRTH OF THE FEDERAL RESERVE

Creation of Central Banks

Because of its influence to shape geo-political and economic events, Globalist's efforts to establish The Federal Reserve, thus gaining control of our money supply, was the first area of influence they sought. Once control of the money supply is established, then the Globalists can shape fiscal and monetary policy to direct the citizenry to accept the gradual tilt towards socialism. As Baron Rothschild once said: "If you want to get control of people, first get control of their money." It is the first and most important also because once accomplished, the other areas in which to gain control and thereby introduce socialism become easier to attain.

What is the Federal Reserve? How did it arrive in the United States? How did the US operate financial markets before its inception? What exactly does the Federal Reserve do? How does it decide what it does? Has the Federal Reserve been good or bad for the United States? What are some of the consequences of its decisions? How many member banks are there in the Federal Reserve System? How many members on its committee, how many Chairmen? With the power the Federal Reserve welds, can anyone recite the names of all the Chairmen of each Federal Reserve Bank, as law students do when recalling the names of the Supreme Court Justices?

The evolution of the Federal Reserve System in the United States has been a long tedious process. During the early years of the United States, many attempts were made by European influences to establish a central bank and were repulsed. So, over time, with failed attempts, drastic measures had to be brought upon the US to overcome the detractors of the Central Bank. The following is a brief history of the attempts and the severe measures used and the organizations founded to perpetuate the system.

The original purpose of the Federal Reserve System, established in 1913, is to give the country an elastic currency, provide facilities for discounting commercial paper and to improve the supervision of banking. (1) However, over the years and through the Globalists sinister plots, added responsibilities include balancing the flow of money to stabilize the economy by infusing money to foster growth when necessary and to slow the economy down to prevent inflation by removing money from the economy; in short, to provide steady growth in the economy and to prevent boom and bust cycles. Additionally, to maintain a high level of employment, to stabilize the purchasing power of the dollar and to maintain reasonable balances in transactions with other countries, have come to be other responsibilities placed upon the Federal Reserve.

As is generally accepted, different cultures and countries came into contact with one another through exploration, trade commerce, and wars. For survival of a country or prevention from becoming extinct and literally being wiped off the face of the earth, countries needed money and natural resources for weaponry. It was through trade where transactions for goods, spices, etc, generated wealth for nations. It was during this time in the 18th Century that a new term of "Merchant Banking" arrived. It means to finance the trade or exchange of goods between countries. One actually loaned money to a ship's Captain to purchase goods in a foreign country so that Captain can return to his country and sell to the public, minus a commission for the "Merchant Banker." The "Merchant Banker" extended credit to facilitate the trade of raw goods and materials. Now one asks who are these Merchant Bankers, and how did they get started?

To oversimplify, names such as Rothschild and Warburg began in Merchant Banking in the 1600's. How? They started because of a Christian edict. (2) Money lending and merchant trading/ banking were considered by Christians to be low brow; and the edict stated it was illegal to transact business on Sundays. The laws of the day did not allow them to learn a trade and become craftsmen, and with no religious constraint for Sunday transactions, the Rothschilds and Warburgs became the Merchant Bankers for Europe. While the Rothschilds had been established long before the Warburgs, after Napolean left Germany, the Warburgs nurtured a business relationship with the Rothschilds in trading silver. (3) This jump started the Warburgs banking prominence. The other major European banking families include the Barings, Lazard, Erlanger, Schroder, Seligman, the Speyers, Mirabaud, Mallet, Fould, and most prominently, Rothschild and Morgan. One can discern the powerful families representing the powerful countries of Europe; Great Britain, France, Germany etc.

One of the Merchant Banking founding fathers is the Warburg family from Germany. Moritz Warburg married Charlotte Oppenheim and of their several children, they had four sons who became prominent international bankers: Max, Paul, Felix and Fritz. Max managed the Rothschild banking operation in Frankfurt and was later Head of the German Secret Police in World War One. Paul trained in the House of Warburg in Germany and later joined Kuhn Loeb in the United States and even later was the lead man in devising the Federal Reserve. Felix married Jacob Schiff's daughter. Mr. Schiff had married Solomon Loeb's daughter Therese, where the firm later adopted his last name and became Kuhn Loeb and Schiff. Felix later accepted a position in NYC office of Kuhn Loeb and Schiff. (4) Managing the merchant transactions, these bankers amassed wealth. As the Warburg family illustrates, as the banks grew, family members branched out into other countries to develop European trading posts and members of merchant banking families also inter-married.

As trade, travel and commerce spread, the world began to shrink in terms of fighting wars, defense and survival. Mutual trust and prosperity were enjoyed by the Merchant Bankers in Europe. When countries and governments needed money, the cabal of international Merchant Bankers was more than willing to provide the loan. When Kings needed money to fight certain wars, they asked the bankers for a loan to cover the military expenditures. Realizing an opportunity to exploit the situation, the Merchant Bankers took advantage of a desperate King and invoked what has become known as the "Mandrake Mechanism." (5) In return for the loan, the King conceded monopoly rights for the Bank to be the sole issuer of English Bank notes. Here is a good example of a "Condition" the government concedes when desperate for money. The Bank in return also accepted IOU's from the King. The government paid the interest and principle on the loan first by trade revenues and eventually by burdening the public in two ways; by taxation and by devaluing their savings through the expansion of currency which led to inflation. This example is similar to the present day The Federal Reserve Bank in the United States which does the same thing. Trade deficits are paid for when the Federal Reserve increases the supply of dollars and raises interest rates to attract financing from around the world, eventually creating inflation which devalues the dollar. The Fed pays for this by increasing taxes on the US citizens. (For instance, think of yourself managing a credit card account and who has 10 workers generating income out of which you receive a portion in taxes. You use this tax revenue to spend on anything. You exceed your credit limit, demand permission from parents (congress) to increase your credit limit so you can spend more. In order to pay the minimum payments, you ask the 10 workers to work harder and increase their taxes.) Realizing the potential profits, the King lobbied to become and was accepted into this money making scheme. Has anyone ever wondered how and in what business the current Queen of England amassed her family fortune? This "Mandrake Mechanism" reveals how one creates something out of nothing, similar to the Federal Reserve of today.

The first such example was the Dutch East Indian Company, founded in 1602. (6) It created a system of a public debt that allowed the government to borrow from its citizens at low interest rates, much like a modern day central bank. The London based merchants were invited into this group provided they could a secure the Royal monopoly for loans to the government in exchange for the companies of London based merchants a monopoly for trading in the East Indies. So, Great Britain agreed to receive loans only from these merchants and the merchants received in return Government promises that it would not grant more trade companies established in Great Britain to transact business in south eastern Pacific, thereby disallowing any competition in East Indian trade. Essentially, Great Britain and the Merchant Bankers devised mutual monopolies.

Great Britain was late to the expansion and trade game. By 1688, James II of Catholic faith, gained prominence and merchants became fearful of England's return to Catholicism. They partnered with William of Orange and the existing Dutch East India Trading Company and conducted a coup and ousted James II in 1688. After the coup's success, Dutch co-conspirator, William of Orange remained on in the business and became the head of England's Executive Branch. The English absorbed the Dutch financial trading institutions and what emerged was the Bank of England in 1694. (7) During the Seven Year War with the French, the British used the financial means inherited from the Dutch, the credit loans and bonds floated to raise money, to beat the French from India and the Caribbean. Because of the war, Britain's debt grew from 74 to 133 million pounds. (8)

Rothschild went one step further and expanded on this "Mandrake Mechanism" scheme and introduced a theory that became known as the "Rothschild Formula." Simply put, its design is to propel countries into war for the profits they yield by influencing governments through monetary impulses and political pressures. If war time loans generate more money through interest payments than do interest payments during peace time, why not orchestrate wars? If weak enemies exist, loan them money to strengthen their military. If no enemy exists, create one. An example would be Lord Rothschild providing financing and licensing rights to the Germans to manufacture British Maxim guns in 1892. By 1908, a Maxim gun was in every German soldier's hands and WWI was just around the corner. (9) The final objective was to disallow one country from becoming or remain predominant because that brings peace and a reduction in debt. With a reduction in debt, two undesired outcomes for the Globalist will occur: fewer dollars generated from interest payments, and freedom from influences from creditors. This Rothschild Formula also enabled the powers that be to introduce governing bodies like their first attempt with the League of Nations and their successful attempt with the United Nations. I'll elaborate more on this later.

Now that Merchant Banking led to the Central Bank in Europe, what was to happen in the New World? When Alexander Hamilton was selected the first Treasury Secretary, he used as a guide Malchy Postlethwayt's "The Universal Dictionary of Trade and Commerce." (10) Topics reviewed include banking, public debt, taxes and money. Hamilton reached a conclusion about a theory of central banks and the fruitful commingling of public and private money: The Bank of England unites public authority and faith with private credit." Hamilton used as a copy, the Bank of England as established in 1694 by King William III. However, sensing a conflict, he deviated from the Bank of England's model in significant respects: He wanted the US bank to serve the government AND invigorate the economy stressing public benefits without the misperception of it being a tool of a small clique of speculators. However, Despite Hamilton's objectives, it did not mean the Europeans did not attempt to exert their influences on the nascent country.

The Europeans tried to introduce its version of central banking on to Hamilton's directives in the US in 1791. Seeing its dubious direction of this central bank, the charter was not renewed in 1811 mainly because state banks opposed central control. A second attempt to charter a national bank came in 1816, but Andrew Jackson killed its renewal attempt in 1832. By the way, Jackson, who always held fast to the backing of the dollar with hard currency, paid the final installment of the national debt (brought on by the War of 1812) in 1835. He was the last President to do so. (11)

Through increasing subservient press, and through bribing local and national politicians, the European elites could introduce and implement their concept of a central bank in the United States, and head toward world socialism. As the Prime Minister of Great Britain, Benjamin Disraeli in 1844 noted, that the world is governed by very different personages from what is imagined by those who are not behind the scenes. Reginald McKenna, chancellor of the Excheqeur of England in 1915-1916 noted that "The ordinary citizen will not like to be told that the banks can, and do, create money....And they who control the credit of the nation direct the policy of Governments and hold in the hollow of their hands the destiny of the people."(12) If the situation were obvious then, why is it not now?

During the Civil War and Reconstruction through the years to McKinley in 1902, the United States grew financially strong and achieved her first place status as a world power. How you ask? By sound fiscal and monetary policy and an import tariff that generated revenues for the treasury and which protected the workers of this country. Sovereignty was intact. The highest standard of living was achieved. No taxes, No central bank. Complete prosperity. In fact, prior to 1903, the United States enjoyed the highest standard of living. From 1860 until 1912, except for Cleveland's 8 years, Republicans held office and sound protectionism and monetary policy ensured prosperity. In this Age of Reconstruction and Roaring 90's, fostered by protectionism, the US attained and surpassed all other countries in standard of living.

It was during the Civil War that the Globalists, or money elite, made inroads into forming the Central Banking system. By making loans to both the Confederate and Union armies, the state-chartered free banks and national banks made staggering profits. In 1863, Lincoln and Congress created the National Banking System, under the advice of the Secretary of the Treasurer and the northern bankers. This National Banking System became the sole issuer of the new uniform currency. Does this sound familiar to the English trading companies brokering loans with the Queen in exchange for trade monopolies?

The National Banking Act passed in 1863, and a law passed in 1865 levied a 10% tax on state banks which led to their demise. So, in a few years, The Globalists eliminated competition from state banks, initiated a uniform currency, and gave themselves the sole right to issue the currency. By the end of the war, direct costs exceeded $6.6 billion dollars in 1860 dollars. As President Lincoln noted: "The money powers prey upon the nation in times of peace and conspire against it in times of adversity. It is more despotic than a monarchy, more insolent than autocracy, more selfish than bureaucracy. It denounces as public enemies, all who question its methods or throw light upon its crimes. I have two great enemies, the Southern Army in front of me and the bankers in the rear. Of the two, the one at my rear is my greatest foe...corporations have been enthroned, and an era of corruption in high places will follow, and the money power of the country will endeavor to prolong its reign by working upon the prejudices of the people until the wealth is aggregated in the hands of a few, and the republic is destroyed." Oh, wasn't Lincoln shot around this time?

President Lincoln was and remains accurate with that statement. He witnessed it with the Civil War. Did similar situations and outcomes arise from WW1? WW2? Korea, Vietnam and now Iraq? Has the US been declining in stature to the point where it is on par with the European Union?

By the end of the 19th century, after several failed attempts to introduce the central bank, the European elites or Globalists had to take drastic measures. The people who thought The Panic of the1890's, attributed by some to have been caused by protectionist measures, were mislead. The Panic of 1890 was not tariff driven. The McKinley Tariff Act of 1890, named after the future President, restored the tariffs to their original levels, (having been reduced in the1883 legislation, which led to the Panic of 1884) that generated the previous economic surpluses.

What happened is the McKinley Tariff of 1890 restored prosperity by increasing custom duties. Citizens at the time thought some of these surpluses should be distributed to the neediest in the country with free coinage of silver. Cries for "Free Silver" backed (redeemed for hard currency or Gold) were shouted. With six new states added to the Union bringing 12 new senators to Congress, "Free Silver" was going to become legislation. Threatening to weaken the McKinley Act and the tariff provision, these new senators won out and "Free Silver" became law encased in the Sherman Act. It is ironic that Congress threatened to overturn the McKinley tariff, the legislative act responsible for generating the monies for this "Free Silver" law.

Receiving "Free Silver" allows for citizens to take

advantage and exploit the situation. Citizens could actually exchange silver given to them, "Free Silver" for something of value, in this case gold. Treasury supply of gold worth $230 million in 1890 decreased to $177 million by 1892, introducing the panic of 1893, resulting in only $132 million dollars worth of gold by 1894. The value of the dollar diminished, and people "panicked" in 1894 as they sought to maintain their income and wealth by having a run on gold. Despite these panics brought on by irresponsible monetary practices, the US sustained its prosperity and standard of living.

Money

The usage of money in the United States is simple and straightforward. It evolved from the barter system through "Hard Currency" to Federal Reserve notes relatively quickly. Simply put, early colonist exchanged surplus good for needed goods. One group may have excess animal skins but lacks grain for food. They exchanged a certain amount of skins for a certain amount of grain with another group, and the "Barter System" was born. The most famous barter example consisted of Peter Minuit's exchange in 1626 of $24 dollars worth of beads and trinkets for the Island of Manhattan. (13) Another example is John Astor, of Waldorf Germany, making his fortune starting in the mink trade in the Northwest Territories. His great-grand son William built the Waldorf Astoria hotel on Park Avenue.

As the barter system flourished, buyers and sellers agreed to simplify the transaction; establishing a certain set amount of animal skins for a certain amount of grain. The word currency came into being as a means of paying bills. Whatever product was actually used, cows, skins or grain, to make payment, it was said to be currency.

The barter system remained as expansion by frontiersmen continued. Travel distance to cities to exchange goods for hard currency was too great which made it too difficult to use something other than barter. Fighting wars and paying for supplies and soldiers increased the difficulty, so a solution had to be made. Also, inconsistencies in the value of the bartering exchange in different parts of the country caused transactional nightmares. Two mink skins in New York for 8 bushels of grain may get you 15 bushels in Virginia. However, exchanging the value of each for hard currency, silver, made economic sense.

Now, paper money originated in Massachusetts in the 1690's as "Promissory Notes" to pay soldiers when no readily available funds were present. Soldiers were "Promised" to be paid in whatever currency, silver, gold or other goods upon presenting these notes to a bank upon return. Regular people or non-soldiers adopted these notes. To simplify the transactions, silver dollars began to be minted in 1792. The word "Dollar" is derived from a 1518 Bohemian word "Joachimsthaler" to name the silver coin circulated in northern Europe. It is called the "Daalder" in Holland, "Daler" in Scandinavia and "Dolar" in England. As Europeans settled America, the word "Dollar" came with them.

Hard currency, such as gold and silver was used as early as 2,500 BC and became widely acceptable as a means of payment. For one example, gold and silver were universally understood as valuable and as ocean going trading companies emerged, paying in coins that were portable, easy to count and durable, became ordinary means to transact business as commerce spread.

So, in 1863, the National Banking Act established a uniform currency. I sense that payment for much needed Civil War supplies and materials created chaos, and something had to be done. The Government passed legislation that dollars were backed, meaning the dollar bill, once called "Silver Certificates" until 1963, could actually be exchanged for a dollar's worth of silver. It was understood that money backed by silver or gold was called "Hard Currency" because of the hardness. When money was made of gold or silver, or could be exchanged for one of them through paper money, it was called commodity currency because it had intrinsic or real value. In early colonial times when Banks were left with insufficient amounts of "hard" currency like silver to fulfill all the exchange obligations from paper money, chaos spread. When commodity currency cannot be redeemed for hard currency, it is called "Fiat " dollars which means one can literally print all they want and have nothing "backing it" except the hard working tax payer. Today, they are called Federal Reserve Notes and cannot be exchange for hard currency.

Now is the time to merge some realities. Reality number one is Great Britain failed several times to recapture the United States both militarily and economically. Militarily, the theory originates with the belief that having been repulsed twice in the Revolutionary War and in the War of 1812 to reclaim the colonies; the British needed a more subtle means to recapture the colonies. Economically, the European Bankers unsuccessfully tried to impose their concept of a central bank into the United States. President Jackson repulsed one attempt.

Reality number two is at the end of the 19th century, the US was becoming a global economic powerhouse, replacing Great Britain as the leader in wealth and financial dominance; a fact not lost on the British. During this period, the financial capital of the world shifted from London to New York. Great Britain realized, "As goes the US, so goes Great Britain," so an alignment or partnership should be brought to bear. With the possibility of losing their dominant place in world events, the British were not going to allow themselves to drop to second tier status for influencing world events. England looked upon the US like an older but smaller brother looks upon a younger, bigger and stronger kid brother. Sensing inability to continue the plan of world domination; for England is too weak and too old to continue the lead role, they looked upon the US to pick up where they left off. Since Britain is incapable of affording financially and militarily to impose their objectives in an ever expanding world, a partnership with the US is desired. Now all the British had to do was find a means to merge the two countries together, unite them in their cause and perpetuate the operation.

By the late 19th Century, these forces, Financiers, Politicians, and Concepts contributing to world government were coming together. The US was emerging as the leader in the free world. Great Britain, still the leader, was realizing the US will surpass them in the near future. Lastly, the concept of ruling the world seems ever more possible, because, having been denied overtly; the British have found the covert means to accomplish their objective; to partner with the US. The concept to retrieve the US and secure continuity of world domination remains alive and intact. The events at this junction in time are in place.

Even the people are in place. What they need is a person to incorporate and set in motion the final push to succeed. The Globalists found this man in Cecil Rhodes.

Rhodes

In actuality, with two failed military attempts, The Revolutionary War and the War of 1812, the concept to recapture the US colonies and return it under British influences originated with Cecil Rhodes. What the British military failed to do twice, Rhodes originated a plan to do it surreptitiously and presented the concept first. While a vague concept may have existed in the Globalist's heads, both the Globalists and Rhodes shared a meeting of the minds. In football parlance, if the Globalist's represent the team owner, Rhodes was the formidable coach, instructing his soon to be players, (Rhodes Scholars) to carry out the plan.

Cecil Rhodes traveled to South Africa for health reasons in the late 1800's. (14) Attracted by the Kimberly Diamond Mines, he ventured into the business, succeeded, accumulated wealth and was elected to the Cape Assembly, the government of the Cape Colony. Being a successful mediator in politics, Rhodes became Prime Minister of the British Colonies in South Africa. After Great Britain seized control of Cape Colony from Holland and their Dutch settlers in 1814, many Boers, which in Dutch means farmers, felt dissatisfied with British rule and fled inland. These settlements organized their own governments, independent of British rule, in the Orange Free State and into an area after having crossed the Vaal River into a second territory, called the Transvaal. When gold was discovered on these lands in 1884, many British prospectors arrived. When the Boers did not permit the

British settlers to vote, tension arose from the British and escalation of military raids mounted.

Disgruntled at the Boers for not accepting British rule, Rhodes supported the raiding efforts of Sir Leander Jameson. With guns and money donated by Rhodes, the British, led by Sir Leander Jameson planned an overthrow of the Transvaal President Paul Kruger. The anger that resulted aided in the outbreak of the Boer War. After several defeats, British commanders asked for and received reinforcements from the homeland and repulsed the brief successful Transvaal counterattacks. By 1910, the Orange Free State and Transvaal were incorporated into the British province of South Africa. Further British expeditions north of these territories were also captured and Rhodesia, named after Rhodes became a British colony.

After Cecil Rhodes acquired his wealth mining diamonds and gold in South Africa, with the help of the British army, he and other wealthy friends, namely Lord Rothschild, started a society which became know as "The Round Table." Rhodes had presented his Rhodes Scholarship concept to Mr. Rothschild back in 1888 with the main objective to spread the ways of the English empire; the King's religion in place of Roman Catholicism and for the ultimate recovery of the United States of America as an integral part of the British Empire. (15) Doesn't this 'recapture' concept seem plausible? Having amassed territories, either through colonization or capturing other nation's colonies through wars, the British Empire could make the famous claim that "The sun never sets on the British Empire." Now that the biggest civilized nation, the United States, soon to be the wealthiest, most economically and geo-politically powerful nation, loaded with natural resources is no longer part of the British Empire and is free from influences, wouldn't any British official be furious at such a loss? When one thinks of British Territories and British influences under the Victorian Age images of tea, cricket, rugby, golf in India, S. Africa, Australia, come to mind. But not in the USA. The US is the country that "Got Away." Wouldn't any British patriot be irate? Having tried twice through wars and failed both times, what other means did Britain have at their disposal to "recapture" the USA as a necessary means to establish a One World Government?

The group's goal, envisioned by Rhodes and Rothschild, was to follow Plato's ideal. Rhodes favorite professor at Oxford was John Ruskin, a devout follower of Plato. Plato's ideals consisted of: A ruling class with a powerful army; using whatever means to wipe out existing governments; the destruction of religion; the elimination of private property, all the while having the ruling class decide what is best for the populace. (16)

Upon Rhodes' death, attached to his will was a "Confession of Faith which outlined the following: A plan for a secret society for the furtherance of the British Empire, bringing the whole world under British rule and for the "recapturing" of the United States. (17) Rhodes intended to take Catholic missionaries and their territories and inject English Empire ways in place of the Catholic religion. In some sense, one can see the attempts today by nefarious characters altering Catholic doctrine with abortion, gay marriage, etc. The general public has taken for granted the brains of these Rhodes Scholars, but are misunderstood. When Rhodes Scholars profess what is best for the US, the exact opposite happens. This group is for the removal of sovereignty of the United States and other nations through the creation of a union e.g. The United Nation, The European Union, and steering the US towards a one world government and economic system, or in other words, towards socialism. This consolidation of countries into one governing body makes it easier for the few to rule. Too many countries, too many religions and too many cultures mean insurmountable obstacles. It is far easier to persuade and assuage one President than 50 Governors. There is an outward appearance of knowledge, success, and knowing what is right, but there exists a hidden agenda that spreads through the undertow of the top layer of news. Out of this group, but there are others, are the so-called "experts" who profess the way things should be and the public just blindly accepts these brilliant people from top schools and their socialistic agendas.

When Rhodes died, he left most of his wealth for the Rhodes Scholarships where foreign students, usually intelligent and from wealthy and well connected families, to travel to England to receive their two year "Indoctrination," akin to a One World training camp. His scholarships given to American students were to unite the two ruling classes of Great Britain and the United States by attracting the best and brightest from the upper classes attending the elite universities.

To draw an analogy in today's world, substituting oil for diamonds, suppose a Bush family member using their considerable influence to usurp control of the Persian Gulf region for the natural resources, substituting oil for diamonds. Encountering a difficult overthrow, the Bush family member asks the US military for assistance and once gained, reaps monetary rewards. Upon the death bed, this Rhodes like figure in the Bush family endows a scholarship for foreign students to study in the US. When one understands how Rhodes made his money, does one really want to place a value on the prestigious Rhodes scholarship?

Upon returning to their respective countries, the students, like secret agents, would spread the One World goals of world government. The rest of his fortune was left to the Round Table group. By 1919, The Round Table Group interlocked with the Rhodes Scholars and formed the "Royal Institute of International Affairs," RAIS. The returning US students and some British co-conspirators, namely Colonel House, started the sister group in the United States called the "Council of Foreign Relations," in 1921 and which still exists today and out of which many cabinet members and State Department officials must be a member to attain their government positions. By 1929, the CFR moved into their new headquarters at 45 East 65 Street in NYC, right next door to the new governor of New York, Franklin D. Roosevelt. (18) Coincidence?

One example of a Rhodes Scholar and perpetuity of agents is Senator J. William Fulbright. Born into wealth and prominence, Fulbright became a Rhodes Scholar and was on the Foreign Affairs Committee. In 1942, as a forward thinking internationalist, he endorsed a post war international organization, which became the UN. Does this appear to be putting the cart before the horse? Already being "In the Know" Fulbright was promoting this one world governing body before the war was fully underway. Fulbright later established a Rhodes like program which bears his name, the Fulbright Scholar. It is out of these groups that the so called "Experts" conceive and promote socialistic agendas while simultaneously defending past decisions, laws and establishments of socialistic programs developed by predecessors.

These groups receive financial assistance, legitimacy, and policy confirmation from tax exempt foundations. The tax exempt foundations like the Carnegie Endowment for International Peace was set up in 1908, before taxation was passed in the Federal Reserve Act of 1913!! (19) Make sense? If one were a Globalist in 1908, and Taxation is a future part of your plan, wouldn't it make sense to protect your own organizations from taxation beforehand? That is what the Globalist did. They created foundations and insulated them from taxes, thereby perpetuating their ability to use their extensive capital to influence geo-political events. The foundations offer collaborative support on policy issues to their affiliate members in the CFR who are in government positions. The foundations also discredit both politically and intellectually any person, or agency who opposes their socialistic goals.

For instance, during the McCarthy Hearings, Norman Dodd was appointed research director investigating foundations. Studying the first year's notes of the CFR, Dodd found discussions on whether there was any means more effective than war to alter the life of the people of a nation. (20) This sounds similar to a "Rothschild's extension of the Mandrake Mechanism. War offers more rapid change than peacetime. The RAIS applied this principle to getting the US involved in World War I. With World War I started, how does one now get the US involved?

I have outlined Rhodes's desire to form a group of intellectual men, of the wealthy, educated, upper crust, politically connected, and powerful industrialists to continue the English speaking supremacy. However, without US cooperation, their ultimate goal of global domination could not be achieved.

I will show how they achieved this surreptitiously through Rhodes and perpetuated it through his scholarships. They assisted JP Morgan in banking and Rockefeller in industry and thus gained a foothold into American economic and political environments. The British then directed the Americans to undertake the concept of the central bank and introduced the Federal Reserve System.

Realizing the threat to their existence in World War I, Great Britain desperately needed the US to help defeat Germany. Examples will follow that will explain the British role in luring or scheming to force the US into the war. Why? In order to fulfill their goal of world government, and to keep the English speaking peoples and their way of life intact. Also a key reason to partner with the US is to maintain their supremacy, and the British needed the US military and economic might on their side. The first attempt of a world governing body under their control, The League of Nations failed. Their second attempt with the UN succeeded.

The Round Table Group needed a world governing body, a League of Nations, to achieve their goal. However, in peacetime, what country would forfeit several important sovereign rights in exchange for peace by subjugating themselves to the rulings or laws of this League? However, thinking diabolically or Machiavellian like, the Round Table surmised a war, or "Rothschild Job" would accomplish their desired result. By fostering a war, the Round Table Group could "scare" the countries into joining.

When the war is over, countries would join this League to secure the peace. Once the League is established, a socialistic anti sovereign mandate could formulate and spread throughout the member countries. It would be similar to burglarize a home and returning the next day to sell the homeowner an alarm system with change in lifestyle stipulations.

During WWII, examples will reveal the British influence on enticing US involvement which led to the United Nations and their top tier position in global politics. Has anyone ever heard of the "Special Relationship" the British and the US share? Has anyone ever imagined what is meant by this statement? It means for the British and the US to join forces economically, politically and culturally for the benefit of the English speaking Christian world. Since the British's desire is for them to maintain their supremacy in Global society and realizing they could not do it alone, they aligned themselves with and steered the US into a partnership where together they could rule the world.

Who are these people and how did they come together as a group and join with the British/US alliance to have a one world socialistic government? Why are they organizing? What are the objectives? How and when do they meet?

The effort to shift the world towards socialism began in Europe, but in order to achieve their ultimate goal of world socialism, the Europeans had to introduce it to the United States. Attempts began 200 years ago but took root 100 years ago in 1903.

Before I describe the events that follow, I just want to add, that prior to 1903, according to Gill's "Trade Wars

Against America," the United States, while accumulating wealth and prosperity to unforeseen levels that generated the highest standard of living in the world at that time, did not have: An Income Tax, Corporate Tax, Inheritance Tax, Capital Gains Tax, Social Security Tax and did not have a Federal Reserve Bank and most importantly, did not have a national debt. Now in just a short 100 years, we have all these taxes, supposedly to make life easier for all and to provide for general welfare, roads, schools, defense etc. Yet despite all these revenue mechanisms for the US Treasury, the United States has watched its' national debt soar to over $5 trillion dollars in 100 short years, and watched personal savings and standard of living drop precipitously. How and why did this happen? We have witnessed stock bubbles and crashes, both of which the Federal Reserve was designed to prevent.

Now, if you were these powerful elites, how would you destroy this young country's supremacy in the world and introduce socialism. You would somehow have to remove the economic policies that provided for this economic juggernaut, and introduce means to gain control slowly of the monetary and fiscal policy of the United States. In order for this to happen, the Globalists needed to gain control of the banking system and they did this through the introduction of the central bank which led to the Federal Reserve System. In order to legitimize the introduction of a central bank, some sort of financial chaos as previously mentioned needed to happen. If some financial catastrophe occurred, the Globalists could then introduce their concept of the Central Bank to restore order to the financial markets and to prevent this crisis from reoccurring.

Think of a seesaw analogy. Imagine the US sits on the high end of the seesaw and the other countries, or the rest of the industrialized nations, are on the low end. The powers- that-be want the seesaw to correct to a level position, which means the US has to suffer in the lifestyle department while the "others" can get off the ground. The US is too powerful financially to allow it to go it alone in global geo-politics. In order for the Globalists to restore some European prominence in world affairs, and to achieve their one world government, the US end of the seesaw would have to be lowered so the other side could rise. Exerting financial and political influences to lower the US end, the Globalists began their process of manipulation, creating a balance where future control of both sides of the seesaw could be engineered by the few powerful elites.

Another method to socialize is using trade to infiltrate powerful populated nations to lure them in. This way of thinking explains why the US is more concerned with China than Cuba. Cuba will eventually fall into the NAFTA/CAFTA web. China, beside economic potential, is the United States version of the Pacific region, the number one country in the third region. This theory falls in line with The European Union and Europe comprising Region One, The United States and NAFTA/CAFTA countries comprising Region Two, and China and the Pacific Rim countries comprising Region Three. This group needs China to be the leader in the third region like Europe needed the US for Region Two.

Why? What is the motive of these powerful men and women who make up the Globalists? Simply put, a group of powerful wealthy individuals want to control the natural resources, geo-political events and simplify the financial and banking interests with regard to trade, taxes and human welfare for self enrichment and socialistic one world government. They want to create three "Super States" comprised of the European Union, the Americas and the Pacific Lands. Each of the three areas will have its own currency, the Euro being an introduction, and accomplish all this using Free Trade as a vehicle to spread their philosophy, retain corporate profits, and suppress any challengers to their agenda. How did this happen?

The NAFTA and CAFTA are the means as we are currently witnessing, and the Pacific Rim Trade agreements are forthcoming. The British attempted to reacquire the United States militarily in two wars. Having failed twice, the British realized exerting economic and political influences on the United States will slowly erode the sovereignty of the US and begin a partnership for Global domination. It was during the turn of the 20th century that two forces, the Globalists and Cecil Rhodes met and joined forces. If the Globalists acted as the team owner, the young Rhodes coached the concept to his scholars, (players) and got the operation underway.

The banker's ultimate goal is to create a world financial system putting control in private hands to dominate the political system of each country and the economy of the world as a whole. The Central Banks would act in concert, by secret agreements and seek to dominate governments by its ability to control Treasury notes, influence the level of economic activity in a country and to reward cooperative politicians that furthered their objectives. The super rich bankers are out to take over the entire planet doing it through socialistic legislation when possible, but using

Communist revolution when necessary. President Bush invaded Iraq. Is Iraq a stabilizing influence in the region designed to protect Israel and the Rothschild elites? Did Bush have a choice, or was he forced to succumb to the Globalists' significant monopoly on the financial operations of the US to push the us into war? Remember what Rothschild said about control of the money and control of the people!! Any similarities to Rhodes and the Boer War?

THE FEDERAL RESERVE; HOW IT WORKS

The original purpose of the Federal Reserve System, established in 1913, as sold to the public, was to prevent boom and bust cycles, (See Morgan induced Panic of 1907) to give the country an elastic currency, provide facilities for discounting commercial paper and to improve the supervision of banking. Elastic money means the capability to infuse or remove the money supply in circulation, based on current economic conditions, either into or out of the economy. Additionally, a high level of employment, stability in the purchasing power of the dollar and to maintain reasonable balances in transactions with other countries have come to be other responsibilities. The Federal Reserve has also extended its realm of responsibilities beyond its original design and as examples will show, the results of these actions were opposite of its' original intent.

Because of its potential ability to influence to shape geo-political and economic events, Globalist's efforts to establish The Federal Reserve gaining control of our money supply was the first area of influence they sought. Once control of the money supply is established, then

Globalists can shape fiscal and monetary policy to direct the citizenry to accept the gradual tilt towards socialism. As Baron Rothschild one said: "If you want to get control of people, first get control of their money." It is the first and most important goal also because once accomplished, the other areas in which to gain control and thereby introduce socialism become easier to obtain. Throughout this section, I wish the reader to remember the words below, their respective definitions and recall them when applicable during the understanding of events.

The evolution of the Federal Reserve System in the United States has been a long tedious process. During the early years of the United States, many attempts were made by European influences to establish a central bank and were repulsed. So, over time, with failed attempts, drastic measures had to be brought upon the US to overcome the detractors of the Central Bank. The following is a brief history of the attempts, the severe measures used, and the organizations founded to perpetuate the system.

The Federal Reserve is actually limitless with the amount of money it can create. For instance, in times before the Federal Reserve, if a bank has $100 dollars worth of gold in its vault, only $100 dollars can be removed (legally) from the bank. When the Government removes that gold "backing," what becomes of the value of the dollars? In the Wild West, when a Cowboy could walk into a bank and exchange his wages from a cattle drive for silver and gold coins, it meant something. Today, these same customers cannot. Since the customer receives nothing in exchange, the dollar and the value of the dollar must be supported, backed by something else to give it its value. In today's world "Backed" usually infers backed by the taxpayer. When this happens, it is said the dollar's value "floats" usually against the values of other currencies.

The Federal Reserve Banking System is comprised of 12 regional banks with the major influence resting in the New York branch. Based on the Federal Open Market Committee evaluations of the economy, it instructs the Fed to tighten or loosen credit. When inflationary fears approach, tightening credit means to shrink the money supply; to remove the amount of dollars in circulation, which slows the economy. To jump start the economy like in 2001, loosening credit means adding money to the economy, to increase the amount of dollars in circulation so consumers can expand the economy.

There are three methods to achieve either direction; Buying/Selling securities, Increase/Decrease the interest rates, and the less widely used adjustment, adjusting the Reserve Requirement.

When inflation (Too many dollars chasing too few goods) approaches, to slow the growing economy, the 12 Federal branches sell Government Securities, i.e. Treasury Bonds, Notes and Bills from member banks. Member banks include nationally chartered and some state chartered banks. Member banks use deposits or money supply in their respective banks to buy these Securities thus decreasing the amount of money to lend to consumers. For economic recovery from a recession, the reverse is true, the Fed buys these Securities from the member banks, adding cash to these member banks for them to lend to consumers to expand the economy. They also lower rates so consumers can afford to pay the interest on borrowing money. Besides lowering rates, lowering the reserve requirements provides more money for loans would work.

The second method to adjust the economy is to raise or lower the discount rate, or interest rate charged to the consumer on money. A consumer wants a loan for a house, and will pay 5% interest on a loan. When the Fed raises the interest rate to 6%, this consumer may think twice because of the increase in cost for the loan and not buy the house, thereby slowing the economy.

The third and not frequently used is the reserve requirement which stipulates the Banks must retain a percentage of deposits in cash. For instance, with a 10% Reserve Requirement for a $100 dollar deposit, the bank must retain $10 dollars allowing for $90 dollars to loan to consumers. The 10% requirement can be adjusted up or down. Here is where I think the Globalists don't want to tread.

The third method of adjusting the reserve requirement is seldom used, because of its limited benefits for the Globalists. If Reserve Requirements were increased providing for less money to be loaned at the same interest rate, the economy would slow down. Imagine a vending machine filled with soda. The Feds decide how many cans to put in the machine and how much to charge for each can. To tighten credit, they decrease the amount of cans in the machine and raise prices, both beneficial to the Gloablists, because they receive more dollars by charging more (Interest Rates) for fewer soda cans. If Reserve Requirements were enacted, fewer cans would remain in the machine but would be unavailable for sale. The price would remain the same, yet consumers could not purchase them. This would slow the economy. The Fed does not want this because they receive no money for the potential sale of available soda. When a vending machine runs out of a selection, the consumer waits for a refill and pays the same price for the soda. The delay slows down progress, slowing inflationary concerns. If the machine is refilled with soda, yet the price increases, doesn't this allow for the wealthy to get wealthier because they and not the poor are the one who could afford to pay higher rates?

Why do Globalists want this? The Federal Reserve uses the first two methods for two reasons: They enrich themselves and maintain their position of socio economic and geo- political influence; and create a two tier class system. By enriching themselves, they can manipulate the masses and further their socialistic goals, and by creating the two tier system, the Globalist can perpetuate the need for someone, the poor, to perform the manual and menial labor for them.

However, these objectives have not entirely been met. Examples will follow that show how these Central Bankers have manipulated the finances of Nations for their own selfish goals with no regard for the people. Evidence will prove that Federal Reserve policy has actually done the opposite of its original design. It has enabled the financing of government deficits which has led to inflation, diminished the value of the dollar, and initiated the necessity of taxation in all forms and sizes. These reversal of intentions have fostered more and increasing taxes, higher unemployment, duel income parents to make up for the decreased purchasing power of the dollar and less disposable income from higher taxes and the subjection to government dominance over everyone's lives. All these actions increased the national debt, which has grown to such high proportions, future taxpayers will work like slaves just to pay the interest. The government buys and pays for whatever it wants by financing it through these "fiat" dollars. These dollars are just printed and no longer backed up by gold, but the good faith and credit of the taxpayers.

The first two methods accomplish several results. One, they both are used to collect more dollars for the Globalist, first by having banks use money to buy the Securities from the privately held Federal Reserve, monies which go into the Globalists account, and secondly, by charging consumers more in higher interest rate payments to borrow money. Secondly, it achieves their desired goal of two classes, by increasing the divide in wealth; for only the wealthy corporations and individuals can afford to borrow at higher interest rates, thus shutting out the lower class from the opportunity for business growth, economic prosperity, individual development and independence. The first two methods help the upper class in the upper class while simultaneously it keeps the lower class in the lower class.

The banker's ultimate goal is to create a world system of financial control in private hands to dominate the political system of each country and the economy of the world as a whole. The Central Banks would act in concert, by secret agreements and sought to dominate its government by its ability to control Treasury Notes, influence the level of economic activity in a country and to reward cooperative politicians that furthered their objectives.

FEDERAL RESERVE

The Federal Reserve's control of our money supply was the first and therefore the most important means to control the populace. By controlling the money supply, you control the people. As Baron Rothschild one said: "If you want to get control of people, first get control of their money." It is the first and most important means also because once accomplished, the other areas in which to gain control and thereby introduce socialism become easier to obtain. Throughout this section, I wish the reader to remember the words below, their respective definitions and recall them when applicable during the understanding of events.

Cartel: A written agreement between belligerent nations, combination of independent commercial enterprises designed to limit competition, a combination of political groups for common action.

Cabal: A number of persons secretly united to bring about an overturn or usurpation especially in public affairs.

The evolution of the Federal Reserve System in the United States has been a long and tedious process. During the early years of the United States, many attempts were made by European influences and were repulsed. So, over time, with failed attempts, drastic measures had to be brought upon the US to overcome the detractors of the Central Bank.

In order to create the Federal Reserve, the aforementioned "chaos" was needed to create a real yet engineered crisis and convince the public the only method to prevent another financial crisis was to have a Central Bank. In 1907, Jacob Schiff of Kuhn Loeb & Co., warned of financial chaos if a Central Bank were not instituted. On a side note, this is the same man who invested millions in the Bolshevik Revolution in Russia in 1917. (21) Why would he do that? Easy, besides making money the revolution could overthrow the crown, thereby dismantling Russian Sovereignty, and socialism and even better communism could be introduced. When Schiff's warnings went unheeded, he had Paul Warburg, from the Rothschild allied banking firm of The House of Warburg, visit the United States and meet with the leading banker at the time, J.P. Morgan. JP Morgan and Company actually got its start in London in 1838 under the name of George Peabody and Company. Morgan, having apprenticed in London under Peabody, returned to the United States and became the "agent" in America for the International Bankers. Paul, a partner in Kuhn Loeb and a representative of the Rothschild banking operations in England and France, ran in the same circles as Morgan. His brother Max managed the family operations in Germany and the Netherlands, his other brother Felix was married to Jacob Schiff's daughter. After convincing Morgan to instigate the Financial Crisis of 1907, Congress, under pressure to restore order, passed the National Monetary Commission headed by Nelson Aldrich. The Senator's daughter married John D Rockefeller Jr. who had a son named Nelson Rockefeller who was Vice President in 1974. Understand the perpetuity? In any case, suspicion by citizens and congress caused further delay of establishing a Central

Bank and the powers-that-be met in secret and devised the plan.

What resulted was the Panic of 1907, a Morgan induced financial crisis. Morgan caused the Panic of 1907. During the summer of 1907, Edward H. Harriman, William Rockefeller, Jacob Schiff and Henry Clay Frick wanted $25 million to stabilize the prices in the marketplace. Morgan, while in London, cabled that "It would be unwise, entirely at variance with all the policies we have adapted being at the head of a declared Stock Exchange manipulation." In the early 1900's, national and state chartered banks could not do Trust business. Seeing an opportunity, Henry Davison of First National Bank and Thomas Lamont of Liberty Bank, (both Morgan employees) set up Bankers Trust to handle the Trust business. The Trusts speculated heavily in questionable investments, Copper Mining being one of them, and unfortunately backed their investments with stock securities as collateral. When rumors spread that Morgan was investing in a new Alaskan Copper mining operation, thereby producing a glut in Copper, the stock skidded 35 points that day which started the ball rolling. (22)

Hence Des Griffin, the author, points out the US plunged into a monetary crisis that had all the earmarks of a "Rothschild Job." The ensuing panic financially ruined tens of thousands of innocent people across the nation while making billions for the banking elite. The purpose of the crisis was two-fold: 1) to make a financial killing for the insiders and 2) to impress on the American people the "Great need" for a Central Bank.

As a result, Morgan literally professed an omnipotent Wall Street money trust was needed. The country needed an elastic currency and a permanent lender to offset these sharp declines in money supply that tended to create severe recessions.

President Roosevelt signed a bill in 1908 implementing the National Monetary Commission to develop a monetary system to prevent this panic from happening again. Remember this; Roosevelt intended the new monetary system to prevent financial disasters from happening again. Senator Aldrich of the Banking Commission was enlisted to travel to Europe. Accompanying him on this two year and $300,000 dollar trip was a close associate of the House of Morgan, George Perkins. Upon his return, Aldrich set up plans to travel south to Georgia and meet with the bankers.

The conspirators met on Morgan's private estate on Jekyll Island in 1910. (23) Participants included Aldrich, Morgan, Abraham Andrews, Assistant Secretary of the US Treasury, Henry Davison, a senior partner in The House of Morgan, Paul Warburg, of the Warburg Bank and their US affiliate, the Manhattan Bank. Thus, representatives constituting 25% of the world wealth from the banking houses of Rothschild, Morgan, Rockefeller Warburg and Kuhn Loeb were meeting in secret to discuss the monetary overthrow of the US. In effect, they were establishing a monetary cartel, much like OPEC's oil cartel. This cartel wanted to increase profits by reducing competition. Their big inner city banks were losing business to rural small state banks and to corporations who were financing expansion by re-investing their profits rather than paying the high interest loans from banks. The conspirators left the island settled on five agreements. Number one is to reduce the competition from smaller banks. The big city banks the Globalists managed were losing potential business to the rural country banks popping up in the expansionist west. Number two is to make money more elastic, or remove the backing of the dollar from hard currency such as gold and silver. This would enable them to create the "Fiat" dollars at will allowing for extreme fluctuations in the economy, a boom and bust capability. The broad reason why is to coerce masses to follow socialist directives of Globalists; we will provide the Fiat dollars to your country in exchange for your government to do this!! Number three: Pool and control the member banks. This is a logical progression of obtaining control. Number Four: Convince Congress to cover any unexpected losses through taxes. Lastly, convince the public, thereby aiding in convincing Congress, that central control over the banking operation would lower interest rates, aid industrial growth and protect the consumer from any economic downturn brought on by any irresponsible bank making risky loans.

When understanding logical progression of these five objectives, the Globalists established the means to dissolve the solid foundation and value of the dollar, create money to foster their means to achieve goals, incorporate into their control, all member banks so no stray bank could divulge their machinations; and to have the gall to pass laws to have taxpayers, instead of themselves to cover their losses. Lastly, convince the public that the controlling machine they devised for their, not the public, benefit will be managed by them.

The significance of 1913 is that the Globalists finally succeeded in the destruction of the capitalistic system as it was designed that made the United States a world power and succeeded in implementing their system of capitalism which serves their small controlling interests. They seized control of the finances, banking and taxation of America, a veritable financial coup d'etat. It removed a legitimate form of financial operation and inserted a controlling, corruptible form.

Anti Central Bank sentiments rang out. Congressman Lindbergh, father of the famous aviator, remarked that the act created the most gigantic trust on earth and legalized the invisible government of monetary power. A New York Times Magazine article reported that Congressman Louis McFadden, Chairman of the House Committee on Banking and Currency from 1920-1931 stated the passage of The Federal Reserve Act brought about a super state controlled by international bankers and international industrialists acting together to enslave the world for their own pleasure.

By gaining control of the banking system, the elites can dictate fiscal and monetary policy, which in turn controls the general public, and once the money is controlled, the Globalists can start controlling the education, and health care and all other aspects of society. Once established, the Federal Reserve Board can pull the strings of the money supply much like a puppet, at will and in either financial direction, economic expansion, or ruin; the elasticity the Globalists sought. Karl Marx understood the importance of centralizing credit in the hands of the state. The Communist Manifesto even calls for the creation of a centralized bank. Lenin agreed that creating a Central Bank was 90% in communizing the country. Reginald McKenna, Chancellor of the Exchequer of England in 1915-16 and Chairman of the board of Midlands Bank of England told his stockholders in 1924 "I am afraid the ordinary citizen will not like to be told that the banks can, and do, create money. And that they who control credit of the nation direct the policy of Governments and hold in the hollow of their hands the destiny of the people." (24) When this elasticity is applied to the utmost, potential drastic economic conditions can occur. Depriving people of the basic necessities will force them to follow the directives. The carrot and stick routine. When economy flourishes, the Globalist can usually pass socialist legislation; people turn a blind eye to legislative regulations and laws because the economy is good. It also allows for the Globalist to set up for a financial crash. So a new step along the ladder towards socialism can be achieved. Remember, small steps over time go unnoticed. Creating a "Chaos" supply is the Socialistic solution. Think of today's credit crisis/foreclosures and stock market decline and potential solutions. More in final thoughts.

To achieve their goals, the Globalists cannot alter life from 1907 to 2007 overnight. Small incremental changes, unnoticed alterations in financial legislation, taxes, trade, economic activity, all contribute a small step in the larger view. In the seesaw example, the steps are small enough alone to go unnoticed, but when looked at over time, one sees the balancing, or leveling off to make for a one world system.

At the outbreak of World War I, the United States, despite the negative effects of the Underwood Tariff of 1913, was still an industrial juggernaut; having nearly 36 percent of the world's total industrial output, far more than any other two countries combined; Germany and Great Britain placed second and third with 16 percent and 15 percent respectively. (25) Despite France's and Russia's vast natural resources they combined for under 12 percent. So, one gets a clear picture of the enormity and power of the US economy. However, just prior to the war, in 1914, the economy suffered mightily. The Underwood Tariff of 1913 combined with the Federal Reserve had sent the nation's industrial leaders into a panic. The Bradstreet Journal reported the largest number of business failures than previously recorded. Andrew Carnegie wrote President Wilson describing he has never seen conditions like this for debtors to pay. Financial conditions were so horrendous, that by July, the New York Stock Exchange, which kept its' doors open during the 1907 panic, did in fact close its doors. Where was Mr. Morgan this time? Why and how did the Federal Reserve, designed to prevent such disasters like Roosevelt had intended, allow this to happen in its' first year of existence? So, if the economy was booming up to the outbreak of WWI, how does one explain this financial disaster, at the same time as industrial output? Simply put, the war production disguised the financial ruin of many and delayed and cushioned the blow of what could have been an even worse disaster.

By 1914, the Globalists had introduced the Central Bank, the Federal Reserve System and taxation. They had control of all facets of fiscal and monetary policy; what they needed was control of the political system. They needed control of the political system so the Globalists could rebuff any challenges to the workings of the Federal Reserve; to prevent a repeat of Andrew Jackson's non-rechartering action.

Shortly thereafter, the Globalist's, weary of public

suspicion about the Federal Reserve, taxation, and the custom duties decline in revenue, all of which brought the economic collapse, needed control of the policy making branch to legitimize the Federal Reserve. To bring about the need for a world governing body and to divert the minds of the suspicious populace, what was needed was rapid change and nothing but war brings more rapid change to achieve their goals. Remember the Rothschild Job example!!

What was needed was a world governing body that would destroy/remove the sovereignty of nations and subject it to a World Body made up of men like themselves. Altering the life of the US was this group's goal. To replace a capitalistic society with a socialistic one is their main objective. And they realized a war was faster than more peaceful and gradual means. What they needed was a war.

Geographically, the US, being located in the western hemisphere and without any local competition, i.e. Mexico and Canada, was an isolated island like empire, separated by two vast oceans from Europe and Asia and therefore situated far enough away from European entanglements. However, for the Globalists to form a world governing body that would justify the existence of the Federal Reserve, they needed to involve the United States in the war. However, two concerns confronted the Globalists and its' English led influence on the US. One was that they had to ensure the US entered the war, and secondly, that the US entered the war on their side. The latter concern is the most important and most difficult. Important because the vast industrial resources of the US would ensure victory to whichever side the US joined.

Secondly, the isolationist fervor in the US and its affiliation towards Germany were too strong for England to take lightly. With 80% of the US population voting for isolation, Wilson won re-election in 1916 on the slogan, "He kept us out of the war." What people also don't realize is that by a margin of one vote, as stated on a Reagan Bush re-election booklet, the US became an English speaking rather than a German speaking country. So there were some strong isolationist and pro Germanic sentiments in the US for the Globalist to overcome. What was needed was a means of deception to entice the United States into war. Enter the Lusitanian affair.

The **British**, repeat **British** Liner Lusitania, built to military specifications was being used as a passenger liner. As a US agent for the Globalists, JP Morgan was in charge of procuring and shipping the much needed munitions to England. Aware of the shipments and out of fear of provoking a US entry, the Germans placed an ad in many East Coast newspapers warning the US citizens not to travel on British liners. JP Morgan used his considerable influence with the media, he funded socialist newspapers, squashed the ads and the Lusitania sailed May 1, 1915. (26) As First Lord of the Admiralty, Winston Churchill ordered a recall of the destroyer escort and slowed the liner down to three fourths speed ensuring an easy and vulnerable target. The rest of the story everyone knows, but what many do not is that the director of the inquiry investigating the Lusitania, which placed the blame on the Captain, resigned from the British Justice system in disgust, commenting years later, "The Lusitanian case was a damned dirty business." Here is an example of the Globalists in both Great Britain and the United States scheming to involve the United States in the war. By aligning the two countries together, the Globalist could pool resources; financial, industrial, military and combine the way of life for English speaking peoples, in order to unify the socialist train of thought. It also started the leveling off process of the seesaw.

The financial ramifications of World War I were dramatic. The national debt of $1.2 billion in 1916 swelled to over $25 billion by the end of the war in 1918. On a per capita basis, the debt rose from $12 per person to $242. The economic situation worsened because the Federal Reserve's money making tactic of raising the discount rate from 4 to 7 percent failed, so the post war recession began in the summer of 1920.

How did World War I benefit the Globalists? It increased the national debt of countries. It increased the taxes needed to pay for the debt. It increased the interest paid on loans to rebuild war torn countries. The central banks under Globalist control collected this money. It furthered their goal of world government by having convinced the citizens the Federal Reserve and taxes were necessary, temporary the citizens thought, but necessary to pay for the recovery and it lent credence to the League of Nations.

To review from 1901 to the end of World War I, The Globalist achieved many of their goals. From the time when McKinley was President and no Federal Reserve, no taxation, no federal debt nor a world governing body, to 1920, when the Globalists pushed through all of these measures to further their goal of world government/socialism. They established a Federal Reserve where the government could spend/loan money to whomever creating a debt, financed by the new income tax on citizens, lowered tariffs which hurt US businesses, increased the debt thereby lowering the value of the dollar. However, their first attempt of a world legislative body, the League of Nations failed.

Tired of Wilson and suspicious of the League of Nations, which the US Congress did not ratify, the public voted for Warren Harding in 1920. What these powerful elites do is create chaos to introduce their socialist plots. They tried with the League of Nations after World War I to foster world government. However, old fashioned Republican Party standards of fiscal conservative and protectionist measures won out.

Harding won in a landslide with over 60% of the vote. What succeeded in extricating the US economy from the post war recession orchestrated by the Federal Reserve was the passage of the Fordney-McCumber Tariff Act of 1922. This undid the disastrous effects of the Underwood Tariff of 1913 which prompted the business failures and Carnegie's letter to Wilson. The duties on iron ore and steel, which had been eliminated in 1913, were restored. The tariffs on sugar, wool and textiles were all increased. With the enactment of the tariff, an economic resurgence followed. Enhancing the prosperity, Andrew Mellon, Secretary of the Treasury, lowered taxes. Combining the tax cuts which spurred growth, and with an increase in custom duties, Mellon achieved a budget surplus year after year and reduced the war debt by almost an third by the end of the decade. These sound fiscal and monetary policies led to an era of unprecedented prosperity. Anyone remember the roaring 20's and the life of Gatsby?

This success and anti world government raised eyebrows and was viewed as an assault of the banker elites.

Something had to be done to defame the Protectionists politicians and their policies. So, the Globalists engineered the Crash of 29, but not before they sold and reaped millions

The Stock Market Crash of 1929 was not brought on by the Smoot Hawley Tariff as the "Experts" profess in history texts and everyone believes. The Smoot Hawley Tariff was enacted eight months after the Crash. (27) What occurred was simply a blowing up of a bubble and then popping of it as orchestrated by these Globalists. Post WWI, Great Britain's economy inflated more than the US. To create parity between the two countries, Britain convinced the US to inflate its economy. The Governor of the Federal Reserve System, Benjamin Strong and the Governor of the Bank of England, Montagu Norman, conspired and convinced Secretary of the Treasury Andrew Mellon to implement two monetary policies. One was to monetize the Fed, (increase the supply and circulation of money) which he did by adding about $2 billion dollars by 1927 along with reducing the discount rate from 4 to 3.5 percent. Both initiatives allowed commercial banks to loan more dollars. In the years from 1923-1929, the Federal Reserve inflated the money supply by 62% creating and infusing the economy with about $11 billion "fiat" dollars. All that was needed now was to pop this expanding bubble. The Federal Reserve accomplished this in August of 1929 by raising the discount rate to 6 percent and simultaneously selling securities in the open market. Remember the example: Raising the discount rate forces the banks to pay more to the Federal Reserve. By offering Bonds with higher interest rates, the Fed forces the banks to buy these Government Bonds, paid by deposits, decreasing the amount of money for loans. Selling securities also forced the banks to buy, use the deposits to buy the Government Securities. Both actions remove money from the economy and people are negatively affected.

Both policies shrank the money supply and tightened credit and the Crash of 29 ensued. Here is another example of how the Federal Reserve manipulates the monetary policy at will and against the wishes of elected officials. It is also another example to use to criticize the Fed and ask how and why this happened when the design of the Fed was to prevent this economic roller coaster from ever happening. This is very similar to Alan Greenspan manipulation of the monetary policy when he blew up the bubble in the late 1990's which allowed for the Tech Bubble Crash which began in the summer of 2000.

The Federal Reserve, in its infinite wisdom, cut the money supply by a third between 1929-and 1930. This decrease in money supply only prolonged the recession and ultimate blame rested on President Hoover with campaign slogans of the recession is "Hoovering" over us.

Now that the Globalists created the financial mess, "One of their own" could be elected. Enter Franklin Roosevelt. Doesn't any one think it strange, that an organization like the Federal Reserve, supposedly designed and implemented to prevent these booms and busts cycles allowed the Crash to happen? As they will tell you, it was the Smoot Hawley Tariff that caused the Crash. But how could the tariff have been held accountable for the Crash, when the tariff was passed nearly six months after the crash?

The crash allowed the money trust to elect their own socialist Franklin Roosevelt. Remember, Roosevelt lived next door to the just formed Council of Foreign Relations, the United States version of the British group Royal Academy of International Studies. Both were outgrowths from Rhodes' dictum. He contributed to the socialist regime by initiating his social programs.

All the attempts to revive the economy failed and promotion of the New Deal failed. Devaluation of the dollar failed, restoring the dollar to gold failed. The failure of the Federal Reserve to pump up inflation with lower rates failed. The Keynesian theory of deficit spending failed. With spending on social programs the country fell further into debt. The buying power of the dollar declined and never regained itself to anywhere close to pre-depression levels. In 1935 alone, the government expenditures were more than the US had spent collectively in the first 124 years of its history up to the creation of the Federal Reserve in 1913. This enormous influx of "Fiat" dollars worsened the already disastrous situation. In 1930, the federal debt was 17.9 billion, mostly from WWI expenses. In ten short years, the national debt in 1940 had grown some $35 billion to more than $53 billion dollars. These expenditures devalue the dollar, encumbering even more the burden to pay for these expenses on taxpaying ability of the citizens.

Since the first attempt of a governing world organization, the League of Nations, failed, a second attempt was needed. Getting the United States involved in World War II was imperative for the Globalists to achieve the world government.

Now, Hitler was an evil man, but the world did not know of his atrocities until after the world was in fact at war. In a 1940 Gallop Poll, 83% of the population was against entering the war. Hitler did not devise his extermination of the Jews until January 1942 during the Wansee Pact, after the war was well underway. (28) The US did not enter the war because it was attacked by Germany, or because of Hitler's atrocities. The US stopped oil exports to the war-mongering expansionist Japanese. Think of the "Dutch East Indies," "French Polynesia" Spain's influence in the Philippines, Great Britain in Singapore. How would you feel if these European countries were colonizing in your back yard? Wouldn't you like to colonize some of the land near your home country before it is all grabbed by Europeans? In retaliation, Japan bombed Pearl Harbor. Many articles have been written that Roosevelt knew of the Pearl Harbor attack and let it happen. The Japanese did copy the British aerial attack on the Italian fleet in Taranto. The British air attack removed the German naval presence from the middle of the Mediterranean, freeing up British shipping in the Mediterranean to supply desperate British forces in Egypt. After Pearl Harbor, The US declared war on Japan; Germany declared war on the US first. It was a tough task for Roosevelt, because the isolationist fever ran rampant throughout the US.

By the end of the war, the federal government spent a total of $387 billion dollars, 95% on the war. The national debt of $43 billion in 1940 soared to $270 billion by 1946. The war ends and their goals are achieved. First, they achieved in this war what they failed to achieve in the First World War; a world governing body. In June of 1945, President Truman signed the United Nations Charter, a euphemism for One World Government. As James Warburg, the son of Paul and the founder of the CFR, remarked to the Senate floor in 1950, "We will have world government, the question is whether we will achieve it through conquest or consent." (22) Secondly, they cemented the relationship between the Federal Reserve and the Treasury, where interest on these war loans are still being paid.

How did the UN affect the US? One objective of the Bretton Woods Conference, where 700 delegates from 44 nations met to formulate a one world government, was to reduce the obstacles of international trade. Organizations that originated from the Bretton Woods Conference include the International Monetary Fund, The World Bank, and the General Agreement on Tariffs and Trade, a predecessor to the WTO. Under the auspices of these money lending institutions, the lending was to be used to promote peace generated by economic prosperity resulting from said loans. Now that the finances of nations had become controlled through Central Banks and has taken root, item number two, Trade, was the next objective of the Globalists.

Secondly, financial contributions to the IMF were based on the Marxist principle of "From each according to his means to each according to his needs." Since most of the world was relatively broke because of the war, the United States paid the lions share for this to work. One other aspect that came out of the conference was the term "scarce." This meant when a currency was in high demand, mainly the US dollar, it could be called "scarce" because of the persistent trade surpluses. The US stood alone in the "scarce" category until the trade deficits appeared in the 1970's.

In 1959, the Council of Foreign Relations in the United States prepared a paper titled Study number 7,

Basic aims of US Foreign Policy in which the US is urged to build a new "International Order, and to increase the authority of the UN. In Dec. of 1961, columnist Edith Kermit Roosevelt, granddaughter of Theodore Roosevelt wrote for the Indianapolis News that the CFR viewpoint is as follows: "The best way to fight Communism is by a One World Socialist state governed by 'experts' like themselves. The results of these policies have been the gradual and ultimate surrender of United States Sovereignty to The United Nations." Douglas MacArthur, upon his return from Korea was amazed and deeply concerned about foreign influences. He observed the extent to which orientation of the United States national policy tends to depart from the traditional courage, vision and forthrightness which have animated and guided our great leaders of the past to be now largely influenced and in some instances to be dictated from abroad and dominated by fears of what others may think or others may do.

However, unlike previous post war eras where custom duties paid the debt, the WWII debt reduction plan to pay the war debt lasted only two years, 1947, 1948, and removed a paltry $17 billion from the $270 billion debt. Because of the Cold War, and Foreign Aid, the debt reduction program was forgotten. Taxpayers merely acquiesced in paying more money in taxes for the eternal interest due bankers and other lenders while the value of the dollar declined first at home and then abroad. How many people, who were alive during the initial phase of Globalist's operations during the World War I, 40 years previous, were still alive to reject these machinations? Not many, or too few to protest. So citizens just accepted the policies from these "Experts." Small steps, small steps!

As Arthur Schlesinger mentions in "The Future of Socialism," 'There seems to be no inherent obstacle to the gradual advance of socialism in the United States than through a series of "New Deals."

So, in 20 short years, from 1925 to 1945, a gigantic leap realistically with an economic boom of the roaring 20's followed by a depression decade 30's followed by 5 years of war, the powers that be orchestrated a depression, and then orchestrated a war. This is the "chaos" implemented by these people which brought three sure fire ways to dismantle the US. The depression, which the Federal Reserve was designed to prevent remember, fostered the means to tax and the reasons for social programs. Secondly, the War fostered the means to have a one world government in the form of the United Nations, and lastly, the side effects included continued spending, higher debts not being paid by customs duties and trade sanctions which dismantle the US's industrial base, all funded by the unknowing US taxpayer.

As the second world war drew to a close, the capitalist class in Western Europe was under severe threat from an upsurge of working class radicalism, the management of which required a strategy more sophisticated than conventional repression, and the first steps were taken, by political parties of both left and right, to develop 'corporatist' programs based on a kind of national protectionism. By contrast, in the USA, the war had brought to dominance an internationally-oriented capitalist class who saw very clearly that their interests lay in a thorough 'liberalization' of the world market, abolition of tariffs, dismantling of sovereign nations to foster a three hemispheric world. Only the false wisdom of hindsight could make the eventual Atlantic Alliance system that emerged by 1950 seem preordained by 'objective' historical forces. Indeed, so accustomed have we become to hearing phrases like 'American imperialism' and witnessing US interventions throughout the world that we can forget just how difficult it was for this internationally oriented fraction of the American capitalist class to impose its agenda upon the US state: the deep-rooted tendency of American political culture has always been what Europeans call Isolationist' and it took extensive political work to drag the Americans into these foreign entanglements. They succeeded in effecting the integration of the Western European capitalist class into a new Atlantic alliance system.

The European Group which traces itself to the Illuminati is called Bilderbergers. They have become the European counterpart with the RAIS, the Trilateral Commission and Council of Foreign Relations.

Bilderberg takes its name from the hotel, belonging to Prince Bernhard of the Netherlands, near Arnhem, where, in May 1954 the first meeting took place of what has ever since been called the Bilderberg Group. (23) Think back to the King William War and the buy out of The Dutch East India Company!! While the name persisted, its meetings are held at different locations. Prince Bernhard himself (who, incidentally, was actually German not Dutch) was chair until 1976 when he was forced to resign because of the Lockheed bribery scandal. The possible significance of this group may be gleaned from the status of its participants: the membership comprises those individuals who would, on most definitions, be regarded as members of the 'ruling class' in Western Europe and North America. In particular, the conferences brought together important figures in most of the largest international corporations with leading politicians and prominent intellectuals (in both academia and journalism).

I - Bernabe, Franco - Vice Chairman, Rothschild Europe

USA - Boot, Max - Neoconservative, Council on Foreign Relations, Features Editor, Wall Street Journal

TR - Dervis, Kemal - Member of Parliament, former senior World Bank official

USA - Donilon, Thomas L - Vice-President, Fannie Mae, Council on Foreign Relations

I - Draghi, Mario - Vice Chairman and Managing Director, Goldman Sachs

USA - Geithner, Timothy F. - President, Federal Reserve Bank of New York

I - Giavazzi, Francesco - Professor of Economics, Bocconi University; adviser, World Bank and European Central bank

GB - Kerr, John - Director, Shell, Rio Tinto and Scottish American Investment Trust, former secretary of European Constitution Commission

USA - Kissinger Henry A. - Chairman, Kissinger Associates Inc.

FIN - Lehtomaki, Paula - Minister of Foreign Trade and Development

FIN - Lipponen, Paavo - Speaker of Parliament; former Prime Minister

INT - Padoa-Schioppa, Tommaso - Director, European Central Bank

So one can see some of the world's most powerful, wealthy men, representing leading global corporations and industrialists, are on the list and meet to decide the fate of the world, all for the benefit of themselves and at the expense of the common man. Please note our current Chairman of the Federal Reserve, Tim Geithner, is on the list. This list is from a few years ago as well, giving Mr. Geithner ample time to be indoctrinated by the Globalists!! Didn't everyone, politicians, the media, claim Tim is the "only" man who can handle this crisis at the time during his confirmation? In a land of 300 million people, if the US's outcome rest on this one man and that is all we, as citizens, can find to solve our issues, it does not speak highly of our financial network.

Later American participants included Robert McNamara, US Secretary of Defense under Kennedy and Johnson (earlier chair of the Ford Motor Company, and later President of the World Bank); and McGeorge Bundy, who worked on the Marshall Plan, was US National Security Adviser and later special foreign policy adviser to Kennedy and Johnson 1960-65, and became President of the Ford Foundation 1966-79. His brother, William Bundy, was with the CIA 1951-61 and later managed the CFR journal "Foreign Affairs" from 1979, after working at the Pentagon 1964-69. He married the daughter of Dean Acheson, Truman's Secretary of State. By the way, Mr. Acheson is also the man who devised the American/British/Dutch oil embargo towards Japan that cut off nearly 95% of oil shipped to Japan. Acheson devised the "Chaos" and then developed the lending institutions to remedy his problem!! Finally, all three Directors of the CIA in this period were also members of Bilderberg: Allen Dulles (Sec. of State John Foster Dulles's brother), John McCone and Richard Helms. Needless to say, all these figures were also members of the CFR. Was it this group that came up with the "Domino Theory" that led the to the US involvement in Vietnam?

The $17 billion dollars Marshall Plan did revive Great Britain and Europe but it also strengthened socialism throughout Europe and through their revitalized industrial bases. It was the carrot and stick routine. Loans will be made to re-industrialize each country's manufacturing base, but socialist tenants must be accepted for a loan to be made. Through the aforementioned trade liberalism provided by the Bretton Woods agreement, countries were allowed to begin their "dumping" of products into the US market. The argument for this plan was to permit access to US markets so the countries nascent manufacturing base could make money so the country could re-pay the Marshall Plan loan. In 26 short years, these policies drove down the trade surpluses until the first trade deficit appeared in 1971. This had two negative side effects. With dwindling surpluses, taxes had to rise to make up for the shortfall which helped pay for government operations. Secondly, with raising trade deficits, the value of the US dollar declined, which effected inflation and higher interest rates.

One other example of Federal Reserve meddling occurred during Truman's presidency. With high taxes, offset by the still high purchasing power of the dollar, and non defense spending reductions, the federal deficit remained relatively low, less than $18 billion for the three years of the Korean War. Because returning World War II soldiers were flush with money and because of the GI Bill, citizens were eager to return to productive lives, and they were. Despite all this, the Federal Reserve wanted to raise Interest Rates. Why??? Just like post World War I.

Truman and the Federal Reserve argued until an accord was passed on March 4, 1951. Eventually, the Federal Reserve issued discounts and advances to their highest level since 1928, thereby ending the boom of the post war years. Think back to the explanation of the machinations of the Federal Reserve; the Globalists will raise Interest Rates when consumers can afford it. They will explain it is necessary to slow the economy when all they are doing are reaping higher profits. A less drastic and softer measure in this case would have been to increase the seldom used Reserve Requirement. This would have kept the Interest Rate at the same level but would have removed more money available to loan, so a consumer would be turned away from a loan by the scarcity of the dollar, not the higher rate.

A Department of Labor statistic in May 1955 reported 156 "distressed areas with high unemployment, 119 more than in 1953, and due mainly to the rise in imports.

Another unforeseen result of the US dollars floating in Europe was the raid on the US's gold stock at Fort Knox. The year 1958 was the first time that dollars held by foreigners exceeded the value of the gold in Fort Knox. This means if foreigners holding dollars want to redeem their dollars for gold, Fort Knox did not have enough Gold in reserves to fulfill all the exchange requests. (31) With deficits increasing, the dollar's value declined and since the dollar was pegged at $35 dollars and ounce, Europeans were taking their new found money from the Marshall Plan, and exchanging them for gold in Fort Knox and selling it at a profit in the open market.

When Kennedy took office in 1961, the short term liabilities owed to foreigners was slightly above their value, estimated at $17.8 billion in gold left in Fort Knox. To restore confidence in the US dollar, Kennedy should have proposed to break away from the Bretton Woods agreement and revalue the US dollar to a more realistic price other than $35 dollars an ounce.

With vast accumulations of dollars floating around the world through trade, aid, military assistance and other illicit means, any more attempts to siphon off the remaining gold would have been disastrous. The game would have stopped. Thus, the Central Bankers devised "Euro Dollars" and they circulate as an international currency. Loans in Euro Dollars began in 1958 and in 1963, the London merchant bank of (guess who) S.G. Warburg underwrote the first Euro Dollar Bond, for a $15 million dollar highway in Italy. (32)

Let's review. A hard working tax paying US citizen has his taxes raised, watches as the value of his dollar depreciates because there are so many of them spread under the auspices of the Federal Reserve and other lending institutions that a foreign bank uses these excess dollars for a loan to another foreign country (Italy for instance) and then receives interest payments from the Italian taxpayer. All this originally financed and continually financed by the US taxpayer.

Carroll Quigley, History Professor at Georgetown, Princeton and Harvard wrote in his 1966 book, "Tragedy and Hope," that "The history of the last century shows that advice given to governments by bankers was consistently good for bankers but disastrous for governments, businessmen and the people generally. Such advice could be enforced if necessary by manipulation of exchanges, gold flows, discounts rates and even levels of business activity." Has this scenario changed since 1966? One can witness the examples of Federal Reserve manipulation in WWI, the Crash of 29, WWII, and the Gold debacle. The boom and bust cycles were supposed to be prevented with the advent of the Federal Reserve,

In comparison, by 1968 the federal debt approached $350 billion or $1,727 for every man, woman and child in the US, whereas, in 1910, the per-capita debt was only $12.41.

With the first trade deficit of $2.3 billion realized in 1971 followed by a $6.4 billion deficit the next year, John Connolly entered the Group of Ten Finance Ministers meeting in Rome with a prescription to revalue the dollar and of the other countries currencies. This reevaluation was to make the US products more affordable to countries to import, or put another way, to make our products less expensive to export, thereby reducing profits for domestic corporations. This attempt and three other attempts under Connolly's successors, one under George Schultz, and two under Paul Volker all failed. Inflation rose, the dollar depreciated, and the trade imbalance only worsened. Look at the trade deficit today. Since the US consumes more than European counterparts, our export dollars decreased, generating less foreign currency to purchase the US' cheaper (depreciated) product.

In the same year of 1971, probably alarmed by the imbalance in trade, the House Foreign Operation Sub-committee on Appropriations investigated the federal expenditures. The Subcommittee reported that in the 25 post war years, (1946-1971) total federal disbursements amounted to $138,446,200,000. Interest that year to finance all the expenses amounted to $74,434,597,000. All financed by the taxpayer.

Here is an example of how trade policy is linked to monetary and fiscal policy. As a result of the first trade deficit in 1971, which caused the dollar's value to decline, higher interest rates on US Bonds were needed to attract foreign investors to finance the US deficit. Tax increases were needed as well to pay the interest on the foreign investments and to finance federal and state operations. During this period, the oil crisis of 1973 appeared exacerbating the overall economic welfare of the country. With the lag time effect of a few years, these negative economic signs came to fruition during Carter's presidency when Interest Rates were 21%, the highest tax bracket was 69% and inflation reached 11%.

Shortly thereafter, the Oil Crisis of 1973 arrived on the scene and made a bad economy worse. Jimmy Carter was elected in 1976. The trade imbalance decreased confidence in the dollar, so the Federal Reserve attracted foreign investment to finance debt, i.e. to loan to consumers to extricate from recession/depression, by raising interest rates to double digit levels. The Interest Rates reached 21% in the late 1970's. Carter increased tax rates to 70% for the highest bracket to generate necessary government revenues. Inflation rates rose worsening the economy. With lack of disposable income, the economy fell into a severe stagnation/depression.

Post WWII to the present brings 11 presidents, two of whom did not believe in the International Banker's plan to socialize this country and the world. The two had similar economic plans they thought best for the country. They both lowered Tax Rates, and both tried to pay off the debt. Their names are Kennedy and Reagan. One was assassinated and one shot, go figure! Reagan was elected and monetary and fiscal policy negotiations dominated the news. Reagan initiated Supply Side economics, an economic philosophy used by Kennedy in the 1960's and Harding in the 1920's. Supply Side economics theory/belief states that creating more disposable income through tax cuts and lowering the interest rates revives and stimulates an economy. Consumers will use these savings to buy more goods and services, save more, or invest more in stocks and bonds; all of which are good for society. As consumers spend more, stores, restaurants, the receivers of this spending will make more and pay more in taxes. For instance, a store owner makes 50,000 and at a 40% tax rate, pays 20,000 in taxes. However, if Supply Side practices are put in place, and consumers spend at this store where the owner makes 80,000 and pays at a 30% rate, he will pay more, 24,000 vs. 20,000 in taxes. That is 4,000 more for the government. A rising tide does raise all boats. If critics state that lowering taxes create deficits which raise interest rates, well, ask them how did Reagan achieve 20 million new hires and watch as both the inflation rate and interest rates fell while he was running up those deficits? While most of the money causing these deficits was spent on the military, winning the Cold War, many think it was money well spent.

Greenspan, within months of his being elected Chairman of the Federal Reserve in 1987, raised rates, which helped trigger the stock crash of 1987. Conversely, some ten years later, he created a bubble much like the 1929 bubble and kept rates low and then delayed raising them, prolonging the economic boom of the late 1990's.

Creating this bubble made fortunes for these Globalist, and then it was too late when he raised rates in 2000. In the 18 years Greenspan managed the Federal Reserve, two of the biggest Stock Crashes occurred, 1987 and 2000. These crashes happened because of the actions of the Federal Reserve, the same instrument whose inception was devised to prevent these boom and bust cycles.

Another example of Federal Reserve manipulation occurred during late in Reagan's second term and during the Bush I presidency. The Federal Reserve Discount Rate rose to 6 1/2% before the 88 election to 7% in Feb 1989 which hurt Bush by applying the brakes to the economy. Was it Bush's economic policies that slowed the economy, causing the recession that cost him re-election or was it the Fed's desire to make Bush look bad? It was during this period, 1989/1990 that Bush uttered those famous words, "No new taxes," which Democrats used against him, forced him into accepting higher taxes which engineered the recession of 1991-92. By July 1992, four months prior to Clinton's election, the discount rate sank to just 3% where it remained unchanged for almost two years. This economic rebound should have been Bush's second term but the Globalists needed a liberal in office to further achieve the socialistic goals at a faster pace. Consequentially, it rose again to 6% just in time to hurt Bush II six months prior to his election.

The Federal Reserve, in another typical blunder, fearing inflation in 2000, ignored the recessionary sign of an inverted yield curve (short term rates yielding more than long term rates.) Why? How? Think of the movie "It's a Wonderful Life." It would be similar to receiving 50 cents on every dollar exchanged today instead of holding onto your money for another week and risk receiving just 25 cents on the same dollar. Inverted yield curves indicate short term prospects are better than long term prospects. The Federal Reserve then actually took money out of the economy by raising rates. This only worsened the situation as prices, profits, equity values and production all collapsed. The Fed continued constricting the money supply which made the dollar too expensive on foreign markets. Foreign investors hesitated on the uncertain prospects of the US economy and the value of the dollar, so investors did not get lured into investing in the higher interest rates. Thus this lack of confidence caused prices, profits, equity values and productivity to collapse further.

I never really understood or should say did not follow the rationale of rising interest rates during good times. The basic premise is after a rebound in the economy when the financial outlook is improving and everyone is becoming prosperous, the Fed intervenes out of fear of inflation and raises interests rates. Making money more expensive to borrow which slows the economy down in order to keep inflation in check is not entirely the right way. The fed has other mechanisms rarely invoked. With millions of dollars to loan, raising rates just enables the big to get bigger, because they can afford to pay the increase from 4 to 7 percent. Raising rates does not necessarily slow the economy down; it preferentially treats those who can afford the raise. It squeezes out those who would benefit the most and exert more of an impact on the economy, the small business. Raising reserve requirements while keeping rates low would enable the small businesses to receive loans. The banks will have less money to loan out. They could raise their reserve requirements and make less money available to loan so not all the loan applicants will receive money, thereby causing a slowdown. They could achieve this while keeping the interest rates the same. Increasing the money supply and raising the interest rate's only closes the door on the struggling small businesses which need the loans. They are the ones who generate the most hiring and most growth. With high interest rates, money becomes available to those wealthy corporations that can afford it. I look at higher interest rates as what the Federal Reserve (and I like to call it a cartel like OPEC,) will charge because during flush times, wealthy people and corporations can afford to pay. It enables the wealthy to expand at the cost of the budding entrepreneur. To corporations, an extra percentage point doesn't make that much of a difference. They can afford to pay it, payment is tax deductible, and it is "OPM," Other People's Money. They can borrow to gobble up other business for more personal gains. To the small businesses, a fraction of a point makes all the difference between expansion or not. To the cartel, they make more money because people are prepared to pay. hey they made a killing and can afford it.

Why do Globalists want this? The Federal Reserve uses the first two methods for two reasons: They enrich themselves and create a two tier class system. By enriching themselves, they can manipulate the masses and further their socialistic goals, and by creating the two tier system, the Globalist's have perpetuated the need for someone, the poor, to perform the manual and menial labor for them.

These secret meetings remain intact today. The 12 Regional Chairmen are not elected, they are appointed by the President and any approval by the Senate is perfunctory. The minutes and notes of The Federal Reserve

Meetings and the Federal Open Market Committee (FOMC) meetings are kept secret. The public is not allowed even to review the discussion in these meetings. Why? If this group decides how to operate our money supply, then why can't the public read about how they arrived at their decision? What are they hiding from the public? Why? What are the Globalists afraid of revealing to the public?

Some of the Globalists objectives are as follows.

Several commentaries took to task Jerry F. Hough of Duke University and the Brookings Institution for backing world government in a June 30 article published in The Los Angeles Times titled "Ethnic Self-Determination Doesn't Deserve Support." Ryan quoted Hough as calling for the "creation of a common European Community that begins at Vladivostok and sweeps west to California" with "one billion of us living together in peace in a huge community with different languages and cultures."

Ryan said such a "community" would force America to "scrap our Constitution and cherished independence." He also wrote that the Bush administration is pushing on a parallel track toward world government by "moving fast on one big "Free Trade" zone without boundaries from Canada and Mexico through all the rest of the Western Hemisphere." The United States, Ryan said, would be "submerged" in the world government envisioned by Bush, and the Globalists, the Bilderberg and Trilateralist groups, and by their propagandists like Hough.

The Free Trade Area of the Americas if enacted would include the entire Western Hemisphere except for Cuba until Fidel Castro is gone. It would then evolve into the "American Union" as a carbon copy of the European Union.

An "Asian-Pacific Union" is to emerge as the third great super state, neatly dividing the world into three great regions for the administrative convenience of the banking and corporate elites. The United States and other international financial institutions should facilitate and administrate these global trade pacts.

Globalists have, for some time, argued for three global currencies-the euro for European Union, the dollar for the American Union and another unnamed- as-of-yet, for the "Asian-Pacific Union."

One Globalist, Kenneth Clarke, a former Chancellor of the British Exchequer, saw the consolidation of currencies as an ideal strategy when he spoke to this reporter, (Ryan) several years ago in Portugal. At that time, Clarke told me that "dollarization" would dominate the globe and "our children will laugh at all the petty currencies we have now."

Resistance in Britain to the euro, and to membership in the European Union, caused much concern and was deemed an obstacle to the solidification of the super state.

As it stands, Europeans can only select members for the European Parliament but not the EU Commission, the bureaucratic powerhouse of the union. Why? Selected like the Globalist's organizations?

The significance of 1913 is that the Globalists finally succeeded in the destruction of the capitalistic system as it was designed that made the United States a world power and succeeded in implementing their system of capitalism which serves their small controlling interests. They seized control of the finances, banking and taxation of America, a veritable financial coup d'etat. It removed a legitimate financial operation and inserted a controlling, corruptible one.

Hopefully, this section has shown the reader the general acceptance by the US public of the few people who control our destiny, the Globalists. Reading this has shown examples how the Globalists have installed their financial machines to control our destiny. They have instilled into the public's minds the subservience to these machinations, swearing obedience and accepting their perpetuity. This socialistic playbook of the Globalist with regard to financial control over our lives is complete, embedded, entrenched an inextricable.

TRADE

"**We cannot afford to have cheap labor in the United States.**" These are the words of President McKinley. A sensible interpretation of these words is that during these times in the 1900's, workers needed adequate pay to maintain the standard of living enjoyed and to retain the skilled labor force to produce the products. Threatening to keep wages low, business would eventually force two disastrous results. One is forcing the job overseas to low wage earning countries, and two, it would create higher unemployment, more government dependency, which shrinks the tax base. Both of these conclusions have come to fruition. It was under McKinley's presidency that the United States enjoyed the prosperity that has been forgotten. Forgotten are his protective tariffs that fostered growth in the US's industrial and manufacturing base, which increased employment, and led to the highest standard of living in the world at the time. He achieved all this without the Central Bank, or Federal Reserve System, without an Income Tax and for that matter without any other form of tax, be it inheritance, corporate, real estate etc. Under McKinley's leadership, the US became the number one country financially, politically, and economically, enabling it to jump into first place and assume its' leadership position among nations in the world. All this I might add **without** a Federal Deficit. Just think about this, because in 100 short years, The Globalists, utilizing their manipulative instruments of the Federal Reserve, the Income Tax, and the reduction in tariffs, have introduced socialism and witnesses should be able to observe our once imminent position eroding under our eyes while amassing a $5-10 trillion dollar deficit; a deficit those aforementioned instruments were supposedly devised to prevent.

I have shown how the Federal Reserve arrived on the scene, but now I want to reveal how trade and tariff reduction have played their role in the defrocking of the United States and how the Globalist have used these two instruments to aid and abet their plans for a socialist world. Revealing the trade policies over the last 100 years will also show how interconnected they are with taxes and how legally our elected officials do not even play a role in regulating the US's commerce anymore.

Protectionism started actually as a result of the Townshend Act of 1767 imposed by the British. This Act was designed to place import duties on British goods arriving in colonial ports. The British used the tax dollars paid by the colonists to raise revenue so they, the British could spend, and pay for the French and Indian War. (33) In response, the colonists adopted the non-importation agreements which forced the repeal of the Townshend Act with the exception of tea. The Boston Tea Party followed, and then the rest is history. So, on the first Independence Day under the new Union created by the Constitution, President George Washington signed into law the first protective legislation for: "The safety and interest of the people." It is from this date until 1913, that the United States pursued protectionist measures that provided for economic prosperity during periods for over a hundred years.

After the Revolutionary War and with the forming of

this nation came the US Constitution. Responsibility for the origination of the financial and banking system fell into the able hands of Alexander Hamilton. A believer in Malchy Postlethwayt's "Universal Dictionary of Trade and Commerce," a veritable almanac of politics, economics and geography, the book contained articles about taxes, public debt, money and banking. Hamilton wrote into the Constitution examples from Postlethwayt and used this book as a guide and as a foundation for the United States economic and banking system. A proponent of manufacturing, Postlethwayt included an adage: "When you get more of foreign coin, the coin for your native coin is said to be high and the reverse low." By 1791, under these policy initiatives, import duties accounted for 90% of government revenues. Today, the reverse is true, taxes, not custom duties are the largest contributor for government revenues.

As a proponent of Postelthwayt, Hamilton included such measures into Washington's first inaugural speech: "A free people should promote such manufactories, as tend to render them independent on others for essential, particularly military supplies," How applicable is this situation today regarding oil? Instead of drilling in the US, providing for our own energy needs, we pay billions to overseas tyrants and rogue countries, Putin's Russia, and Chavez's Venezuela, who in turn use these dollars to finance their aggression towards the western world. Are the Globalists providing an enemy as stated earlier in this book?

When Jefferson entered the White House in 1800, he inherited prosperous times that only improved. Through Hamilton's trade policies, a trade induced boom in tariff revenue allowed for him, Jefferson, to produce a budget surplus.

How well did the custom duties provide for the country? When Jefferson bought the Louisiana Purchase from France in 1803 for a total of $15 million dollars, a $5 million dollar surplus was already in place in the Treasury to be used thanks to the more than $12 million collected the previous year from custom duties. (34) So, the United States doubled in territory without taxes, without borrowing and without war. Another example of custom duties generating enough revenues to cover government expenditures is in 1811, when custom duties accounted for more than $13 million dollars or 99% of the revenue for the Treasury.

In 1861, with almost 95% of the Treasury being funded by custom duties, the year end deficit of $417 million dollars brought on by the Civil War caused some concern. In 1862, Congress enacted a more aggressive means to finance the war, the income tax. This measure did not provide the necessary funds as the revenue collectors had hoped. They realized this idea was counter productive because at every point along the production line, from supplies, to assemblers, to the final product, at every transition, the item was taxed. Each person handling the product added the tax onto the cost for the next handler. Many items were taxed 12 times through the manufacturing process and thus became too expensive. The tax increased the cost of the finished product and sales dropped because of excessive costs. To compensate for these higher costs, President Lincoln passed the "war tariff" or Tariff Act of 1864 which increased the average duty on imports to over 47%. It was this Act which remained in place for the next two decades that fueled the great expansion in agriculture, industry and commerce that amazed the world. It fostered the Industrial Revolution and allowed for the "Roaring 90's." How? The importers paid this custom duty, or tariff, to the U.S. Government for access to the U.S. market.

By 1880, under these protective measures Lincoln put in place, the US surpassed England, which had adhered to its' free trade policy since the 1830's, as the industrial leader of the world. Germany, copying the US's methods, was second, followed by England. (35)

From the 1860's to the end of the century, manufacturing plants increased from roughly 140,000 plants to 512,000 plants. These establishments' employment grew from 1.3 million people to over 5 million employees. These employees' earnings went from $378 million per year $2.3 billion a year and the productive value grew from $1.9 billion to more than $13 billion per year. This is what is needed today; a larger tax base so individual taxes can decrease. You achieve a larger tax base by promoting domestic competition. You achieve more domestic competition by installing a protective tariff and lowering taxes to foster investment.

Thanks to the custom duties of between 40 and 50 percent from late 1890's until the fateful year of 1914, the Treasury was able to afford new expenses inherited from the victory in the Spanish American War. Namely, the US could afford to pay the financial burden of the War, accept the responsibilities of new territory gained from the war, Puerto Rico and the Philippines, and strengthen the Navy and Army for maintaining the US involvement in world affairs. The Treasury could also assume the $400 million dollar construction burden of the Panama Canal from France. Think about this; being able to afford all these new expenses without an income tax. Not a bad situation thanks to the sound economic protective trade measures of custom duties.

There was no personal or corporate income tax. It was not needed. To resolve some confusion in today's world about how tariffs work, an explanation with historical intentions follows. A tariff is more like a traffic toll imposed on foreign companies and countries in exchange for access to the US market. Since most imported products cost less than their US counterpart, because of cheaper labor, the tariffs increased the price to the amount of the domestic item thus leveling off the cost to be competitive with the US prices. This way, consumers could choose between two similar items competitively priced, a domestic or foreign purchase. They could afford both because no taxation allowed for higher levels of disposable income. The Treasury collected these tariffs or custom duties and used this revenue for expenditures, i.e. the Louisiana Purchase. The Treasury didn't need to tax because of the custom duties collected on the imported item. Because of domestic competition, prices remained low. This is how tariffs work and generated the monies for the Treasury while promoting high domestic employment, a larger tax base and prosperous general welfare.

Today it is the other way around. Without a tariff the US is forced to lower its prices to be competitive to the lower priced imports. Manufacturers either slash wages or move to factories off-shore for cheaper labor. By removing the custom duties, the treasury lacks funds, so the Government taxes the people, thereby reducing the disposable income. When one has less money than before, one cannot afford the "now" higher priced US item and must buy the "non tariff imposed" less expensive foreign item. This forces job layoffs, factory closings and the export of jobs. Today, the government calls this outsourcing, it sounds more businesslike and efficient I guess. The impact however is costing jobs, increasing existing taxes, devising new taxes, and a decline in the general welfare of citizens and of the country.

One can witness this from the automobile industry to the sneaker industry. In the early 1970's the first trade deficit brought a decline in the dollar's value, so people bought Toyotas at first because they were less expensive than domestic models. With soaring gas prices, and seeking high mileage cars, people bought more foreign imports which began the erosion of the US auto maker. Other factors later came into play, but the US auto business is not where it used to be, i.e. "As goes GM, so does the US" is no longer applicable. Reducing tariffs is good, proponents like to state; it makes things cheaper and more competitive. So, with a reduction in tariff revenues causing an increase in taxes to make up for the shortfall, people have less disposable income and are forced to buy the less expensive import. It is a merry-go-round. In fact, the tariff reduction is the main culprit of diminishing the US position of economic supremacy among nations.

Historically, it is these protective tariffs which funded the US government for 125 years, up through the McKinley presidency. During McKinley's term, the US enjoyed a federal surplus, low unemployment, a high standard of living and no income tax. The US did not need an income tax because the monies generated by these tariffs covered the expenses of the US government. Doesn't anyone remember the term "The Roaring 90's?" As mentioned in

William Gill's "Trade Wars Against America," it was the Payne-Aldrich Tariff Act of 1909 which slashed the tariffs, most likely under the influences of the Globalists, since no sound reason to lower the duties presented itself, thereby decreasing the amount of money flowing into the Treasury. Shortly thereafter, in 1913, to make up the shortfall in funds, as covered in "Taxes" the government passed the 16th Amendment creating the Income Tax.

How? The fateful event was the Spanish American War in 1898. Because of the war, custom revenues were down so, a 15% Inheritance Tax was imposed to assist paying for the war. Post war, in 1902, this inheritance tax was repealed. In 1900, Congress with McKinley's approval passed the Currency Act placing the US on the gold standard and ensuring the treasury department maintained parity between the dollar and gold; parity meaning an exchange for a certain amount of dollars for a certain amount of gold.

However, with general prosperity and welfare throughout the nation, the Globalist realized that their socialist goal of world government and control of the money supply was slowly losing momentum. Something had to be done to restore their emphasis on slashing the tariffs, forming a central bank, and instituting the income tax. The Globalist knew that McKinley and his protective measures had to go and have him replaced by a surrogate member.

Not much evidence has been found to substantiate a theory, but it is very coincidental that the assassination of President McKinley in 1902 occurred. Enter Theodore Roosevelt. McKinley was shot in 1901, Lincoln in 1865, and Garfield in 1881. All three were strong supporters of protectionism. Coincidence; I think not.

Roosevelt expanded the government, and with expansion comes expenses. However, the expenses grew faster than the revenue stream from custom duties. By 1908, realizing the costs of this expansion, Roosevelt needed more funds, but from where? Sensing suspicions about tariffs creating monopolies, a tariff review was in order. While Roosevelt lowered tariffs, which even provided less money for his expensive and expansive government programs, he attempted to usher in a graduated income tax. However, years before, the US Supreme Court ruled that an **Income Tax was unconstitutional**, so the powers rephrased it an "excise tax." (36)

During the new Taft Administration what followed was The Payne Aldrich Tariff Act of 1909, which, while protecting the workers less, (by cutting the tariffs) also had attached an "excise tax" on corporations, which was in actuality an income tax and a constitutional amendment for a graduated income tax. Most significantly, however, was the provision granting the President authority over regulating trade instead of Congress. In the Constitution, Article 1, section 8 dealing with the Powers of Congress, prohibits the States from levying duties on imports or exports without the consent of Congress, reserving all such rights to the Treasury. This changes the mechanism of trade policy. Whereas the treasury would have examined the revenue stream from custom duties and compared it with economic welfare of the country, it would ask congress to adjust tariffs accordingly. This Act now provided the legal means for the President to usurp this power from Congress and make recommendations and enact trade policy with any country the president chooses. The President was now granted permission over Congress's constitutional right to regulate trade. The shift to a world governing body commences and continues through the remaining century.

In one big tariff measure, Congress and the President accomplished most of the Globalist's goals. The stage was set for the US worker to come under assault from the lower wage earning countries which succeeded in introducing devastating economic affects. They lowered tariffs which sets the stage for business failures and high unemployment creating more government dependency. Lowering tariffs allowed for more of the less expensive imported products to enter, fewer sales for domestic companies, eventual layoffs, increased unemployment as a result and more government dependency. The Globalists transferred control of these tariffs from the legislative branch where it was put by the Founding Fathers, to the executive branch where one person could decide the fate of millions without a vote. Lastly, the Globalists also enacted the confiscatory means of taxation which arrived in four short years; their literal means to reach into a hard working citizen's pockets and steal their money for their causes.

Remember other simultaneous Globalist inspired events occurring around the same time. The Morgan inspired stock crash of 1907, Roosevelt sending Nelson Aldrich on a two year stint to Europe, Morgan preparing for his trip to Jekyll Island. The business failures of 1914 come to mind. All these events occurring around the same time.

As a result, by 1914 custom duties were accounting for a less dominant role in providing the necessary funds for the Treasury. Taxes and increases of them were the only means to make up for the shortfall. An Income Tax, only 1% on income in excess of $4,000.00 dollars for married couples and 6% on income from $20,000 dollars up to $500,000 seemed insignificant, and it was, but the means to increase the taxes was in place and that was all that mattered. What are the rates today, 15, 28, 35 percent!!? What has happened in this country when 1% sufficed and in 100 years, confiscatory levels of 35 and during Carter 70% and Kennedy 90% is not enough?!! It has been proven that excessive taxation only causes inflation; see the example during the Civil War when taxes were imposed to help finance the war. After products were taxed 12 times through the manufacturing process, the cost to consumers was so prohibitive; the taxes were counterproductive and removed.

However, just prior to the war, in 1914, the economy suffered mightily. The Underwood Tariff of 1913 combined with the Federal Reserve had sent the nation's industrial leaders into a panic. The Bradstreet Journal reported the largest number of business failures than was previously recorded. Andrew Carnegie wrote President Wilson describing he has never seen conditions like this for debtors to pay. Financial conditions were so horrendous, that by July the New York Stock Exchange, which kept its' doors open during the 1907 panic, did in fact close its doors. Where were Morgan and his bailout this time?

Then came the war and as previously mentioned; the account does not need to be repeated here.

The financial ramifications of World War I were dramatic. The national debt of $1.2 billion in 1916 swelled to over $25 billion by the end of the war. On a per capita basis, the debt rose from $12 per person to $242. (37) The economic situation worsened with the Federal Reserve raising the re-discount rate from 4 to 7 percent and the post war recession began in the summer of 1920.

What succeeded in extricating the US economy from the recession was the passage of the Fordney-McCumber Tariff Act of 1922. This undid the disastrous effects of the Underwood Tariff of 1913 which prompted the business failures and Carnegie's letter to Wilson. The duties on iron ore and steel, which had been eliminated in 1913, were restored. The tariffs on sugar, wool and textiles were all increased. With the enactment of the tariff, an economic resurgence followed. Enhancing the prosperity, Andrew Mellon, Secretary of the Treasury, lowered taxes. Combining the tax cuts which spurred growth, and with an increase in custom duties, Mellon achieved a budget surplus year after year and reduced the war debt by almost a third by the end of the decade.

In his preface of John Murray's 1911 book, "The Case against Free Trade," Joseph Chamberlain remarked: "Free Trade is the negation of organization, of settled and consistent policy. It is a triumph of chance, the disordered and selfish competition of immediate individual interests without regard to the permanent welfare of the whole."

As previously mentioned, the Payne Aldrich Tariff Act did not cause the Crash of 1929, so I am jumping to post war. Post World War II, Congress worked on the Trade Act of 1934 which among its several provisions allowed for a greater shift in control of trade and tariffs from the legislature to the executive branch. The agreement permitted the president to enter into "agreements" not "treaties" without the "advise and consent" of the Senate and allowed the President to raise and lower tariffs by as much as 50%, powers exclusively reserved for the Congress as stipulated in Article I Section 8 of the Constitution. Much to the chagrin of many, Congress passed a trade extension of the Act, most likely for two reasons, to appease the new President Truman and to honor the chief sponsor of the bill, the late Franklin Roosevelt. Is this similar to honoring Ted Kennedy with Universal Health Care?

On a side note, GATT evolved after the failure to pass the ITO, or International Trade Organization, which was negotiated in the mid 1940's. The ITO plan was concocted at Bretton Woods in 1944 by US Assistant Secretary of the Treasury Harry Dexter White, who was later identified as a soviet agent. (38) The ITO which was to have been under the UN supervision was to have broad regulatory provisions covering trade, business practices, and employment rules. However, under pressure from the business community and concerns about the ITO threatening US sovereignty, the US Congress did not ratify it, and the less stringent GATT was approved. As will later be described, the WTO formation is the fulfillment of the ITO. This is what I mean by slow gradual unnoticed steps towards socialism.

The extension led to the plan to have 50 countries meet in Havana to form GATT or General Agreement on Tariffs and Trade. Concern in Congress ran rampant. Democrat Senator Joseph O'Mahoney of Wyoming commented in Alan Drury's account of the Senate: "How could the Senator from Georgia (Walter George) contemplate without concern in an age of creeping totalitarianism the abject surrender of Congressional control over tariffs? Everywhere the governments of free men are at bay. A great step will be taken toward totalitarianism if Congressional review of tariff reduction is not restored."

The creation of the General Agreement on Tariffs and Trade occurred in 1947. (42) Its aim was to reduce trade barriers with countries.

By 1993, the Globalists needed to expand on GATT for Europe and introduce NAFTA, or North American Free Trade Agreement for the Western Hemisphere. (Notice how these trade "agreements" are no longer "treaties?") NAFTA was to eliminate trade barriers, customs for North America, essentially breaking down the barriers between Canadian and US and US and Mexican borders. The three countries were to merge to become one big trading block....similar to the merging of the European Union.

How can one rational person with common sense believe the US worker can compete with the low wages of Mexico or Canada while maintaining their standard of living? People realize they can't.

Retired entrepreneur and revered financier, Sir James Goldsmith has remarked in his book Le Piege, "The Trap" remarked the expanding GATT agreement forming the European Union will bring social unrest and political instability on a global scale to make 1917 seem insignificant. GATT will transfer jobs from developed to developing countries that will force the poor of the rich countries to subsidize the wealthy of the poor countries. The passage of GATT will eventually plant the seeds to global and social upheaval with the loss of jobs to third world countries. GATT is of no concern to the West, thinking the "Eurocrats" in Brussels have gone mad.

Observing the demise of the once British Empire, with its proud and ubiquitous Navy, slowly deteriorate because of Free Trade, Goldsmith fears any more trade agreements will slowly shift the global power from the West to the third world. What GATT means Goldsmith insists, is that our accumulated wealth over centuries, our standard of living, and way of life, will be transferred to the developing countries like China, who is already building a burgeoning Navy.

Goldsmith further urged that the US cannot grow for the sake of growth, meaning to seek higher profits derived from low wage workers in foreign countries will translate into higher unemployment, crime epidemics, social collapse and drug crises. Non regulated trade will mean our standard of living and wages will be leveled down to the world average. Is this not happening? This is what I mean by the seesaw example.

Sure, companies currently might be making money because of higher exports, so the stock rises and the CEO can trade in his stock options for mega bucks; but at what costs. If a law were passed to share this wealth via the tax free dividend, then every stockholder will realize more disposable income....which is desperately needed now. Goldsmith's final comment is the leveling of wages will be overwhelmingly downward because of the vast growth of underdeveloped populations in the third world.

By 1995, GATT was revised and a stronger world governing body arose, The World Trade Organization. Today, member countries in the WTO number 125. With the advent of the WTO came stronger enforcement powers; rules which affect over 90% of international trade. Critics of the WTO site this controlling interest as an example of a dramatic shift in power from citizens and national governments to a global authority operated by unelected officials.

Before NAFTA was passed in 1993/94, some brief

facts. Since 1980 until passage, more than 600,000 US manufacturing jobs had already been lost to Mexico. Over 2,200 US owned plants employ workers in electronics, TV sets, and automobiles. In fact, General Motors is the largest private employer in Mexico, nearly 36,000 on the payroll while simultaneously laying off 75,000 workers in the US and Canada.

In 1993, William von Raab, Commissioner of US Customs in the Reagan Administration believed there would be chaos on the border in NAFTA passed. Trucks would roll across our borders, illegal immigrants would flood our countries, all because of Free Trade. Sam Francis, a syndicated columnist said to a Congressional Joint Committee that within the nine months of passage of NAFTA, Mexican imports to this country cost the US 137,000 jobs. During the January to June period, the US posted an $8.5 billion dollar deficit compared to a $1.1 billion dollar trade surplus the year earlier.

Within a year of NAFTA being passed, tomato production in Florida dropped 25%. The Scott Paper Company cut 10,500 jobs, and planned to build a $148 million dollar plant in Mexico. All this under the auspices of Free Trade, as we the Middle Class watch plants relocate, communities vanish, jobs disappear, neighborhoods stagnate, and the Middle Class opportunities and hopes for a better future vanish.

Who are these members of the WTO? How many of them are there? All WTO negotiations occur behind closed doors. Why? The WTO dispute resolution panels are comprised of trade representatives from each country and from a set roster. How does one apply for the job? Someone in government who aligns themselves with free trade policy and Socialism is appointed. No Senate approval or oversight? Labor Unions and environmental groups are barely represented. Any small businessman, family farmer, health, consumer or any other citizen group is completely shut out from being on the panel. Does this sound similar to the mechanism of the Federal Reserve Board? What a coincidence!!

Impact on Workers

Free Trade advocates or opponents of Protectionism always like to state that Free Trade is good; it provides for competition, lowers prices for consumers and expands the economy through trade. What this means is that because of higher taxes, consumers have less money for disposable income to spend on the higher priced domestic product, so they purchase the "dumped" and therefore less expensive foreign made product. What happens next is domestic manufacturers go out of business and that shrinks the tax base thereby causing an increase in taxes on the already overtaxed and dwindling number of taxpayers to make up for the shortfall in tax revenue. Hasn't this downward spiral been happening for years?

Free Trade can assist a corporation's bottom line as it has done with the slumping economy of 2008. With deficits lowering the value of the dollar, (making it even harder for US citizens to get by) exports become cheaper for foreigners. The export revenue has offset the domestic downturn. With foreign workers lower wages and export revenue, they have realized a greater profit than if they paid US wages. Great profits lead to higher stock prices where they can exercise their stock options. Have any shareholders realized or received some form of revenue sharing in the form of dividends? Would that help people? Yes! Do citizens get angry watching CEO's make hundreds of millions from corporate profits yet pay under a dollar from profits to stockholders?!! Of course. Make dividend payments from corporations to shareholders tax free!! With nearly 50 million US citizens invested in the stock market, imagine the financial impact on society if these shareholders received a substantial tax free dividend.

Two examples of CEO insouciance appeared in the International Herald Tribune on Sept. 1 1993. The Chairman and principle owner of several corporations in diverse fields mentioned he already had 21,000 workers in Mexico. He would love to see NAFTA pass, so he could save the $11 million dollars he pays in Made in Mexico tariffs, and move more workers to Mexico, where wages are one-tenth of his US employees.

A Michigan refrigeration manufacturer would also like to see NAFTA pass; he would move his whole manufacturing operation to Mexico. What do you think would happen to those middle and low income class workers in Michigan? Without jobs, tax base shrinks, less tax revenues etc. We could be trading Free Trade for freedom he exclaimed.

The positive impact of Free Trade has been taught for so long in University economic classes that no one dares speak out against it. However, in recent years, a growing number of concerned citizens are asking questions about the "myth" of Free Trade.

Protectionism or anti Free Trade citizens believe the opposite is true. They argue that domestic competition had already been in place and foreign competition was unnecessary. Look at the number of automobile and

TV manufacturers the US once had. Secondly, it was this domestic competition, just like what Hamilton said, that kept prices low, not less expensive foreign imports like the Free Traders want one to believe. It was the increase in the confiscatory level of taxes and duty free imports that forced the US consumers to buy the cheaper import. Lastly, the economy shrinks with Free Trade; it does not expand.

A statistic from the US Labor Department states every $1 billion in exports creates 22,000 jobs, so the reverse equation holds true; for $1 billion in imports, we lose 22,000 jobs. So, with an on going deficit, we lose more jobs than are created by free trade. Within this statistic, for every manufacturing job three support jobs are created, supplier, assemblers, salesmen etc., not to mention the professional workers, lawyers, accountants, doctors that rely on these added clients. Conversely, the reverse is true. Think of the recent 30,000 workers laid off recently from General Motors and the impact they have on the local community of businesses and professional workers. Most will lose revenues and some will close, all negatively impacting the tax base.

One of President Clinton's 300 trade deals was the signing over of the Long Beach Navy Base to COSCO, or the China Ocean Shipping Company. Clinton agreed to lease the base to the communist government of China without a national security review. Just think of what enters this base; illegal immigrants, drugs, weapons, undocumented but legal products that hurt domestic producers, disease, sickness etc.

Another example of the negative impact of Free Trade appeared in the New York Times. In the article, Joseph Kahn writes that a "Prominent Congressional

Commission reported the trade deficit has become unsustainably large and dangerous for the economy. The trade imbalance of $30 Billion in 1991 has grown to over $450 Billion this year. Kahn further cites Richard D'Amato, a democratic trade expert who states, "Through Clinton's signing of over 300 trade deals which aren't enforced, the US throws $1 Billion a day out the window." In the same piece, George Becker, President of the United Steel Workers of America states 6 million jobs have been lost to America's one-sided-trade openness. Another publication supports this assertion. The Economic Policy Institute documented that while rising exports created 4.1 million jobs, the surge in imports caused the US to lose 7.3 million jobs for a net loss of 3.2 million jobs, or 64,000 jobs per state. Think of 64,000 layoffs and the impact on local communities, tax base, tax revenue, bank deposits, spending etc.

In a March 16 New York Times article, Alan Greenspan sited several examples of financial woes for the US citizen. The average family debt jumped from $54,000 in 1990 to $79,000 last year, an over 50% increase in 13 years. Public debt, once a small percentage of federal outlays ranging from 9-13 percent from 1940 to 1980, ballooned to 22% under Clinton from 1995-1998.

Greenspan voiced similar concern over the balance of payments or current account deficit which reached a record $531 Billion last year. Like many economists, one of them being from the socialist oracle of Univ. of California at Berkeley, a former Fed Governor named Janet Yellin. She aligns herself with Greenspan by supporting his recommendation to lower the value of the dollar to make exports cheaper and imports more expensive.

What happens if foreigners turn a blind eye to the US and stops lending it money to finance its' current account shortfall. To attract investments, Interests Rates will have to be raised, debt payments increased, and real estate values could fall.

He also remarked that US reliance on foreign borrowing which soared to over 500 billion last year has caused the dollar to decline sharply. Look at November's exchange rates; the dollar is down against every European currency.

In March 22, 2004 issue of Time, a record $43.1 billion trade deficit for the month of January was noted. In the same piece, the value of the dollar declined 44% against the Euro in the last two years. To show the perverse economic theory of policy makers today, this declining dollar was supposed to make our goods less expensive abroad, thereby offsetting or declining of the trade imbalance. The trouble with this theory is that the US does not make much any more to export.

To clarify and to start at the beginning, tariffs historically acted primarily as a revenue generator and workforce protector. In recent times and for a variety of reasons, wages, standard of living, etc., domestic goods cost more than imports. For instance, a domestic made automobile cost $20,000 and an import cost $15,000. A tariff worked, by placing a "duty" of $5,000 dollars onto to the price of the import for two reasons. Historically, it was for access to the US market, like a toll for a bridge or a cover charge to enter a bar. During the halcyon days of protectionism, this "$5,000 duty" was placed into the Treasury, not taxes, for government expenditures. US citizens, with little or no taxes had more disposable income to pay a similar or slightly higher priced domestic product. Remember, the domestic competition also kept prices low. Secondly, it protected the domestic workforce by keeping prices competitive. A price disparity too large would have made the foreign product too attractive to ignore and eventually hurt the domestic workforce. With the removal of the tariffs, this scenario eventually occurred and is continuing.

Over decades, with the removal of tariffs generating less Treasury revenue, higher and more forms of taxation were imposed on citizens. Consumers, because of high taxes and less disposable income began to buy the more affordable less expensive duty free import such as the early model Toyotas or Datsuns (Nissans). Foreign companies price their products below their costs, and "DUMP" them into the US market. Domestic companies lose sales revenue and layoffs follow. Once foreign makers "dump" enough of their product into the US market, the domestic manufacturers are eventually forced to transfer jobs overseas for cheaper labor costs or are forced to close shop. Need I add the loss of Oldsmobile?

Unfortunately, what happens is the US manufacturer is forced to accept pay cuts to be competitive with foreign makers, in complete contrast to good policy. Similar policy concepts occur in most other manufacturing fields. This is what McKinley meant by not affording cheap labor. With lower wages, standard of living suffers, tax revenues decrease, and thereby forcing increases in tax rates, or devising new forms of taxes to make up for the shortfall.

Concerning an article by George Will, in which he asserts that the tariff will destroy 10 jobs in the steel-consuming sector, is false. He also mentions that companies will leave the country to avoid the tariff. The tariff is not imposed on the US companies Mr. Will, so why would they leave the country? What happens because of Free Trade and no tariffs is that the US companies suffer a decline in revenue followed by layoffs because they can't compete with prices from low wages from overseas companies. The US companies relocate as a result of low or no tariffs. How many US plants have moved to the cheap labor of Mexico or the Far East in recent years? He mentions 31 steel companies that have filed for bankruptcy (not to mention other industries) because of the difficulty of competing with a European conglomerate. This is all a result of Free Trade. It is a vicious cycle. Plant closings force layoffs and this reduces tax revenues.

The Labor Department statistic uses a multiplier of one and a half jobs are created for every steel job. When 500,000 jobs are lost, 750,000 other jobs are lost as well. The Chamber of Commerce of Illinois study reveals the multiplier is really over 3 jobs lost for every steel worker unemployed which puts the real number of 1,500,000 jobs lost as well. Again, what does this do to the community's tax base, fewer workers, less tax revenue, harder for state governments to operate, so they raise taxes!!

The burden is shifted to the fewer working people by raising their taxes to pay for the recently unemployed in the name of "Trade Adjustment Assistance." For many years, the US has experienced a trade deficit, and in the last two years, it has been over $400 billion dollars. That is money going out of the country when it should be coming into the US. What does this do to the value of the US dollar? It declines, just as what Postelthwayt said. With this amount of money coming in, the income tax would no longer be needed, just like in McKinley's era. If we drilled for our own oil, we could save and invest the $900 billion dollars we send overseas.

In June 1981, when President Reagan let the OMA or Orderly Marketing Agreement with Taiwan and Korea expire, shoe imports shot up to over 60%. This increased the deficit and decreased employment in the footwear industry in the US from 240,000 in 1968 to under 40,000 by 1982. Sen. John Heinz of Pennsylvania stated in a press conference that "American shoe manufacturers are not losing sales because they are not competitive, unfair trade restrictions on part of other producers have closed foreign markets to American products and made the US the dumping ground for world exports. Sen. George Mitchell of Maine further remarked that 2,000 of his state 17,000 shoe workers have already lost their jobs as a result of the President's free trade policy.

What has happened is Nike pays for cheap labor in foreign countries when the shoes could be made here in the States. Don't confuse costing more to make, with less profit. Labor costs for a domestically made $100 dollar sneaker may be more, lowering the profits for Nike, when compared to the profits made with labor costs in foreign countries. However, Nike needs the profit margin to pay the endorsement deals for Tiger Woods and Lebron James; a sum over $200 million dollars.

Television is another example of how Free Trade destroys our manufacturing base and drives up prices once the TV market is captured by foreigners. The US citizenry is held hostage and pays an enormous sum for these foreign TV's when if built domestically, the competitive market here would have kept prices down. By the 1960's there were 28 TV manufacturers in the United

States. With the decline in the dollar since 1971, due in large part because of the first ever trade imbalance that year, disposable income was down. This made foreign TV more affordable. Japan, under MITI or the Japanese Ministry of Trade, approved a plan to target the high tech US market. They began to dump their TV's on our markets. A $750 dollar TV in Japan was dumped in the US and sold for $295. By 1976, Japan grabbed 75% of the black and white TV market and over 50% of the color market. (39)

An invention of the US, with 28 company names like Zenith, GE, RCA Magnavox, Motorola, Emerson, Admiral, Philco, Sylvania and Westinghouse, the once proud TV industry employing thousands producing competitively priced TV's has now gone by the wayside under the hoax of Free Trade.

No one has tried to calculate the amount of jobs lost to the Japanese trade imbalance. In January 1994, a sampling of foreseeable job cuts amounted to Westinghouse 6,000 jobs, Xerox 10,000 and GTE nearly 17,000. Once formidable companies these companies are hardly household names anymore. What happens to these laid off workers? How many get new jobs at the same wages/salaries? How many need government assistance? What happens to the tax base in these communities?

Foreign governments know it is they that can count on the protection from the US government which ironically denies protection to their own industries while granting it to other countries.

The article provides further proof of the negative impact of Free Trade by instituting what is now called "trade adjustment assistance," basically handing out tax dollars for subsistence. Here is the socializing effect. The Globalist promote Free Trade promising economic windfalls, and what really happens is unemployment rises, and higher taxes are imposed on the dwindling numbers in the workforce to care for the free trade victims. The Free Trade victims also become more dependent on the Government, the Socializing effect, which is exactly what the Globalists want, dependency, and not self reliance.

Another example of high end jobs being outsourced is provided in a July 22, 2004 article by Stephen Roach, Chief Economist at Morgan Stanley. Roach summarizes with his coined term of "Global Labor Arbitrage," which states that because new information technologies have advanced, products, knowledge and consultation in high paying jobs here have moved overseas to lower paying high end jobs. Call for a computer consultation or learn where your x-ray is being read and you'll realize that you are talking to India.

Appearing on the same page on the same day, Senator Schumer and Paul Craig Roberts showcase the pitfalls for Free Trade as well. Put simply, they counter the traditionally held belief of Free Trade as being the cornerstone of economic prosperity as outmoded. At one point a few hundred years ago, Free Trade may have been the logical economic theory. Transporting the "factors of production" the resources to produce goods, timber, soil and people over international boundaries and across oceans would appear illogical and inefficient. Today, with the internet, high tech jobs and even areas in the medical profession are being transported over seas. They mention, as an example of the financial impact on tax revenue lost and the impact on the local economy, how 800 high tech jobs from a major financial firm each earning $150,000 will be shipped over seas. They fear the American worker is facing a new era of direct Global competition. How can the US worker who once earned $150,000 compete against a man in India doing the same task who earns $20,000? Simply, what I just saw in the news is how US workers are accepting less pay in order to keep the job. A story which appeared on Peter Jennings World News Tonight describes a woman who took a $20,000 dollar pay cut in order to keep her job here in the US and not watch it be shipped overseas. This falls in line with a national study that says the US economy is creating jobs but the post recovery pay is about 21% less then the jobs previously held.

Schumer and Roberts both conclude old fashioned Protectionism is not the answer but that a new way of thinking will have to emerge when economist and policymakers end the confusion between the free flow of goods and free flow of the factors of production. I translate this hogwash into to simple terms; these economist and policymakers haven't a clue how to fix the problem. The problem has always been two fold. Either no one realizes the reasons for the dollar's decline and then they make the wrong recommendations to improve the situation or if they do know, they ignore it because remedies would not follow their socialistic goals.

In a March 15, 2004 article in the Hartford Courant, the story tells of two people who have been laid off due to free trade and have had to or are willing to accept a lower paying job. After 28 years of making tools at about $30 dollars an hour or $60,000 per year, Keith Burnham from Michigan is sewing boat upholstery in his garage for roughly $15 dollars an hour. And, yes, with no benefits. Another Michigan resident, Cheryl Dreger complains she hasn't found a job and is willing to take a 30% cut in pay, just to work, but is having difficulty just finding a job. It is one thing to find a job and not accept it because it doesn't pay well, but when people cannot find a job evan a low paying job, then things are really bad.

According to Bob Herbert of the New York Times, the middle class is in trouble. Instead of looking to a brighter future for the next generation, the current middle class is working and struggling to keep themselves from falling into a lower segment on the standard of living ladder. The information age jobs which replaced the manufacturing jobs that were shipped overseas, are now being shipped overseas as well, and are unfortunately not being replaced, despite an improving economy and healthier stock market. The well educated and highly skilled white collar workers are finding it harder and harder to find a job for which they have been trained and for the pay they feel they deserve.

In a more recent article appearing in the NY Times on Nov. 26 2004, Steve Roach mentions weakness is strength. The fall of the dollar "is a logical outgrowth of an unbalanced world economy and America's gaping current account deficit." In reality, the dollar's decline in value has more to do with the latter than the former. The fall of the dollar should not be a "logical" outgrowth of an unbalanced world economy. It results from free, not fair trade policies which have benefited the foreigners at the expense of the US citizens. Remember what Postelthwayt said about more of your own currency leaving your country than other currencies coming in, it is a bad thing......?

Roach furthers states that US consumers are squandering their savings and borrowing against their future to the extent that personal savings rates have declined to just 0.2% of disposable personal income in September. Ever wonder why? As previously mentioned, with less disposable income and a dwindling value in the dollar, citizens need to withdraw from their savings to survive. It is not excessive greed and materialism. It is the basic desire to remain in the lifestyle to which one has become accustomed. Mr. Roach seems to approve of the dollar's devaluation some more, much like what Bush and Greenspan want. The conventional wisdom among the powers-that-be is that a cheaper dollar will make our products more competitive and improve exports thereby decreasing the trade imbalance. Have we not heard this before? Didn't I mention four previous failed attempts at devaluation, James Baker's in 1985, and Paul Volker's attempt before that?

Mr. Roach cites four other reasons to devalue the dollar. First, a gradual need for higher interest rates will attract the needed foreign investment to finance and sustain the growth of the economy. Higher interest rates (cost of borrowing money) would suppress growth in the housing, durable goods, and automobile sector and hinder business capital spending. (These are leading economic indicators and therefore, to stymie these sectors would be bad, not good for the economy.) Roach wrongly assumes with higher Interest Rates, a higher domestic savings rate will follow coupled with a reduction in need of foreign capital investment in the US markets. Higher interest rates slows business spending, another negative on the economy. Good business sense wants businesses to spend, expand and hire more people. Raising rates will only make the Globalists richer by forcing only the businesses who can afford to pay the rate hike, pay the higher rate, while simultaneously closing the door on the less fortunate businesses who cannot afford the hike to expand its' operation and on the consumer who wants to buy a house, fill it with durable goods, purchase a car etc. . Lastly, Roach wrongly insinuates that with higher interest rates, people will save. With higher interest rates, the dollar decreases in value, so people will remove money not deposit money into savings just to get by.

Mr. Roach's second and third convictions about the dollar's fall are intertwined. When the dollar declines, foreign currencies strengthen, and Roach asks for Asian countries to share in some of the burden of adjusting to the dollar's decline. According to Mr. Roach, as stronger foreign currencies emerge, their exports will become less attractive to US consumers, thereby assisting the domestic markets and shrinking the trade deficit. Aren't foreign currencies at historically high levels already while simultaneously the trade deficit reaches a record $665 billion and counting? With this scenario, how can the dollar further depreciate, how can the foreign currency strengthen anymore to improve this disastrous deficit? With this foreign strength, our domestic companies should be enjoying a windfall. What is not happening is tourism. With our currency weak, foreigners should be visiting the US at record levels but lack of popularity has curtailed interest. With a strong dollar, US tourism in Europe helps them a great deal, but US citizens aren't traveling because of the devalued dollar.

While as recently as 2007/2006, exports have risen, two problems remain. One, the exports have not surpassed the imports, so trade deficits remain. Secondly, the export increase does not trickle down to the consumer. The CEO's do well, as do the foreign employees working for US companies, but the US middle class suffers. Are jobs increasing? No. Have any profits been distributed in the form of dividends? NO.

On a smaller regional scale to amplify the larger problem of the global picture, in the state of CT, a recent article appeared on the Op Ed page in The Hartford Courant (April 6, 2004) by Peter Gioia, an Economist with the CT Business & Industry Association. He asserts that global trade, not protectionism, is what is needed to mend the CT economy. Gioia remarks protectionism invites retaliation against those businesses and that what we need as a state is to create a more competitive cost climate for business and to enforce trade agreements so that our companies can compete on a level playing field in the global market. Translation, we as a state and therefore a country must accept unfair rulings by this world group, the WTO, made up of unelected officials that impose restrictions against our commerce and impose monetary penalties to the respective businesses. These remarks also reflect the attempt to lower our standard of living, create a competitive cost climate, to the level of third world countries. The Globalists want to balance the seesaw at the cost of our jobs, our monetary rewards, and our standard of living.

Gioia further points out that $1 billion of CT exports create 22,000 jobs here. That statistic is from the US Labor Department and the reverse equation holds true;

for $1 billion in imports, we lose 22,000 jobs. So, with an on going deficit, we lose more jobs than are created by free trade. He then says how global trade has increased the quality of life. I want to see how. Under more protective measures, with a trade balance in the black, a strong dollar because of it, and lower taxes because of a strong dollar, one parent was all that was needed to provide for the family. Presently, the majority of families have both parents working, and finding it difficult to get by.

I found it very ironic that the day after his article appeared on the OP ED page, an April 7 article appeared in the Hartford Courant outlining the plunge in jobs in the State's Aerospace Industry. There was a colored chart showing the 50% drop in employment in just one industry, from 59,500 jobs in 1990 declining to just 30,300 by today. A reminder that NAFTA was signed in Dec. 1993 and went into effect in 1994. The timing of this important legislation, near the Christmas break resembles the Federal Reserve legislation in 1913!! The article points out an estimate from Steve Prout, president of an aerospace manufacturer, what doesn't bode well for Pratt, doesn't bode well for CT. How? One estimate comments that there are approximately 500 aerospace parts suppliers in CT employing 10,000 to 15,000 workers. That supports the Labor Department conservative statistic that says 2 to 3 jobs are created in supportive roles for every manufacturing job. Therefore, the 30,000 jobs lost since 1990 multiplies out to 60,000 to 90,000 jobs lost in the state in 14 years. And that is just from one industry. Think of all the other industries that have suffered job losses and one arrives at a large number of growing unemployment. This is a true and accurate assessment of the Free Trade myth, albeit a small example set in CT., but I am using it as a microcosm of the bigger picture unfolding across the nation.

News of any job recovery is misleading. From Nov. 2001 through June 2004, private sector payroll has risen a miniscule 0.2%. The hiring in the news is for the low paying low end jobs; temporary agencies, clothing stores, courier services, social work, or non- productive industries. Conversely, according to Labor statistics, reports state that for every manufacturing job, three other support jobs are created, and manufacturing jobs have continued to lag. Roach further comments that between March and June, low end industries which employ 22% of the work force accounted for 44% of the new hiring. In comparison, high end jobs which is the driving force behind greater incomes and consumer demand, account for 24% of the overall work force, but accounted for only 29% of new hires during the same period.

In a recent Op-Ed piece, Bob Herbert describes the American dream of the middle class absorbing the hard working families from the lower income groups. He goes on to remark it is the dream of young people of successive generations doing better than their parents did. Does this scenario still seem true in today's world? Near the end he states no one, the President, Kerry and Edwards nor any economists know what to do. The meat of the article relates the middle class is in trouble. Instead of looking ahead to a brighter future, people are becoming more and more worried about slipping back down the economic ladder of success. The United States, with its' recent outsourcing of high technical jobs, which fill the gap created by the manufacturing and industrial jobs lost to NAFTA and Free Trade, are not being replaced by any new jobs just over the horizon.

In two articles appearing on the same day in the same New York Times outlining the poor performance and broken promises of Free Trade and NAFTA, Joseph Stiglitz, a former Chief Economist of the World Bank and Nobel Prize winner in economics in 2001, points out that the 10 year anniversary of NAFTA has shown no known improvements in Mexico and the United States. He states Mexico grew at an average annual rate of 3.2% per capita from 1948-1973. In the 10 years of NAFTA, the economy grew at a dismal 1%. In contrast, Korea and China, with no trade pact as of yet grew at 4.3% and 7% per capita respectively for the same period. Income disparities between the US and Mexico, once to be eliminated by NAFTA, have actually grown by 10.6%. In 1994 the year NAFTA was signed with Mexico and Canada, the US enjoyed a positive trade balance, or surplus. In the first year of NAFTA, the trade surplus reversed by $16 million dollars to a $15 million dollar deficit and has since grown every year to over $30 million dollars.

On the same day I am writing this, the merger between Fleet and Bank of America has just laid off 4,500 workers.

This appears to be a sign that to the Globalist, everything is going along as planned. Since McKinley stated the US cannot afford to have cheap labor, to the Volker statement that the economy of the US needs to be driven down to the level of the rest of the world.

This is another example of the Globalist's attempt to brainwash and reach into the heads of our economists and policymakers. Think of new and different ways to socialize the world, argue and debate the finer points which will lead towards world socialism but please agree not to invoke the one policy that will redirect and solve the ongoing problem.

Before one can make viable sound correct recommendations, one has to discover the real and hidden reasons for the dollar's decline. With a trade deficit, a country like the US needs to finance the shortfall. The US borrows from abroad with US Treasury Bonds. The money from the bonds pays the interest on previous loans that covered the previous deficits. When interest payments become a large portion of the overall debt, the value of the currency declines. When debt ceilings have to be raised in order to float more bonds to receive more money to pay off an ever increasing interest payments on higher debts, the dollar declines even further. Think of this as a credit card with a credit limit. When the remaining loan amount available is not enough to cover the minimum payment due, an increase in the credit limit enables one to borrow against it in order to make the minimum payment. Congress votes for this increase or the Federal Reserve floats more bonds at higher interest rates to attract investors. This is the major reason the dollar declines and explains the current situation. Remember Postylewaht's remarks of a: "currency declines when more of your country's money goes out than foreign currency coming in."

Personal savings is down because people are trying to maintain their socio-economic position and lifestyle. The dollar's diminishing purchase power (trade deficit related, and Federal Reserve inflationary policies) and excessive taxation has eroded disposable income where people HAVE to use savings to survive and pay for basic necessities and not buy the "wants" on their lists. It is the "wants" of consumer that stimulate even further the economy. In an upward mobile society where people are trying to live the "American Dream" of having a better life than their parents, the citizens of today are finding it more difficult to surpass their parents. Fifty years ago, one parent was enough to get by. Why? Strong dollar, no trade deficit, and less Federal Reserve manipulation. Today, we have huge trade deficits, and the dollar is at an all time low so two parents work to and scramble to get by.

Europeans are irate at the US because the dollar's decline negatively impacts them in two areas. A weak dollar means US will spend less on their European goods; even though there is still a huge trade deficit. Tourism trips to Europe will decline, adding to their troubles. It also means Europeans will look to US companies rather than European companies for products causing a revenue decline for foreign companies. Lastly, the Europeans are going against their financial stratagem and are using some of their savings to invest in our Bonds to cover our expenses.

The bottom line to remedy this is to shrink the trade deficit. This will strengthen the dollar. A strong dollar will allow consumers (with the help of lower taxes to have higher disposable income) to spend more on either domestic or foreign goods with less of their money. Using less of their more valuable money, consumers will increase investments, spending, and spending on other items, the "wants" and increase SAVINGS. With a strong dollar, travel to Europe will increase and the tourist trade will benefit. With Europe benefiting, US tourism will improve. Europeans, instead of spending their savings on buying US Treasuries, should be able to afford paying a tariff which the treasury then could apply to the deficit.

What would be wrong to have Nike shift their employees from overseas back to the US? Pay these workers a decent wage, 10-15 an hour and still sell the sneakers for a $100 dollars. Okay, it will decrease Nike's profit margin so they can't afford the huge endorsement deals, but the employees will add to the economy. What Nike has to learn is they can either pay in taxes to cover the unemployed, or pay a little more and hire the unemployed. With some money, these new employees might go out and buy some of Nike's product. Sounds like Henry Ford's way of doing business; paying his employees more so they could afford his cars. This scenario can happen with most production in the US; Televisions, computers, clothing etc. the list can go on.

If anyone doesn't think this concept will work, just review the Nov. 8th 2004 issue in Time magazine. In it is the story of New Balance, the athletic shoe wear manufacturer. The company is headquartered in the expensive northeast area of the country, Massachusetts specifically, where it has five factories in New England and one other in California. The sales growth of 10-12% over 2003 has generated more than $1.4 billion in sales this year. The average wage is $12 dollars an hour, right in line with my estimate of one weeks wages equal a months rent and what is needed to survive in the United States. Remember what President McKinley said about America not being able to afford cheap labor. In contrast, the Chinese laborer makes .40 cents an hour; hence Phil Knight and Nike record a higher profit margin and can afford to pay those huge endorsement deals.

Jim Davis, owner of New Balance since he bought it 1972, has done something differently than what Nike has done. I am not bad mouthing Nike, just using it as an example. Since the early 70's the US shoe industry has lost almost 200,000 jobs while just fewer than 21,000 remain. Eschewing endorsements deals, Davis has used some of the retained earnings money to increase his domestic payroll by 65% since 1995, adding 500 blue collar jobs.

Think of the impact 500 jobs have on an economy. It may not seem like many when compared to the millions of layoffs, but it is a start. Count 500 people in your neighborhood or in a school cafeteria or classroom and the number of people who are earning $500 a week can make an impact. They are earning a living, able to pay rent or a mortgage. These 500 people are increasing the tax base, contributing to the tax revenue for the town and state, decreasing the burden on existing taxpayers. These added tax dollars enable a town to afford new programs, whether for schools, adult activities, athletic, health care for their communities. These same 500 people, besides saving some of there money, are spending it in coffee shops, bars, restaurants, retail stores, forever increasing the revenues for these respective owners; who in turn, earn more money and therefore pay more in taxes. For instance, if a retail store pays $10,000 in taxes (20% tax on $50,000 revenue) for a net $40K, it will not care for a moment if the store pays $16,000 in taxes (20% on $80,000 revenue) for a net $64,000 dollars. The store owner will gladly pay an extra $6,000 in taxes for an extra $24,000 in their pocket. What does one think the store owner does with an extra $24,000 dollars? The cycle continues.

The extra $6,000 increases the tax revenue for the state and country and that is just one person. This is what Kennedy and Reagan did; a rising tide lifts all boats.

This is also what Bush is trying to accomplish with his tax cuts. This is also an example of how trade and taxes are intricately intertwined.

With a strong dollar peaking in value in March and despite soaring trade deficits, Secretary of State James Baker in Sept. 1985 tried to offset this trade imbalance by devaluing the dollar. He convinced Reagan and representatives from Japan, Canada Great Britain and other large European countries behind a "closed doors" meeting at the Plaza in New York City to devalue the dollar. Much like in today's situation the other countries involved were skeptical because they knew devaluation of the dollar eventually hurts them. Concession were made and are suggested to be made again, namely, not to have the other participants demand higher Interest Rates and to revalue their own currency. Everyone agreed and the Plaza Accord or Plaza Pact was enacted and all thought with a cheaper dollar, US products will be competitively priced in the world markets and exports would increase. This policy, tried three previously times and all resulted in failure, was supposed to foster more jobs, leading to higher prosperity where the US products would become more competitive in the world market and which would balance out the trade deficit. Karl Otto Pohl, the President of West Germany's central bank remarked the day after the Plaza Accord the "change in the exchange rate will generate resistance to the protectionist threat" growing in America and in Congress. One result was by 1986, the Consumer Price Index quadrupled from 1.1% to 4.4%. The $130 billion dollar shortfall in 1984 climbed to over $171 billion by 1987. The devaluation's impact on the dollar was immediate. In the next day, the dollar fell 6 cents in London, 14 pfennings against the Deutschemark and forty centimes against the French franc. In Tokyo, closed for that Monday, opened the next day and the dollar fell against the yen.

The impact domestically makes the purchasing power of the dollar weaken, which forces consumers to eat into their savings, hence the low savings rate presently occurring for the last 20 years.

Following is an example of how these Globalist perpetuate themselves, and their socialist agenda.

In a Dec. 7 2004 NY Times editorial, Jeffrey E. Garten, Dean of the Yale School of Management, and a former economic and foreign policy associate in the Nixon, Ford, Carter and Clinton administration recommends following the Baker Plan in the Plaza Pact.

Garten disagrees with Treasury Secretary John Snow and Fed Chairman Greenspan who believe a 30% decline in value of the dollar is needed to resolve the trade imbalance. Garten is right and I agree. However, Garten's suggestion of the Plaza accord is also wrong. It relies on the Japan and China, the participants this time, to agree on the two concessions vital for this policy to work and unlikely to be accepted this time around. One concession is for the Asians not to demand higher Interest Rates on Treasuries and the second one is for the Asians to go along like last time to re-value their respective currencies. Agreements on both are highly unlikely. It sounds as if we, (the US) that because of our ruinous trade and monetary policies are asking the Asians to alter their successful policies to conform to our failures.

To review, the dollar appreciated 40% from the end of 1980 to early 1984. Conventional wisdom holds higher interest rates were responsible for the dollar's strength. Wrong! Reagan's tax cut took hold and with more disposable income, consumers spent, invested and saved. The interest rates actually declined during Reagan's first term from the all time high double digit levels in Carter's years.

What followed is the strong dollar curtails export growth from companies. It curtailed the growth, not the survival of the company. When the Tax Legislation of 1986 passed, and without tariffs, consumers purchased the drastically reduced or "dumped" imports. This is when a tariff should have implemented. In the automobile example, a $5,000 tariff would have made the foreign car competitively priced and the tariff collected and deposited in the Treasury. The consumer decides between two similarly priced cars. US car sales would slow down, but not to catastrophic levels with forced closures and transfer of jobs. The consumer could have bought the foreign car and have the tariff deposited into the Treasury. Foreign car manufacturer would have benefited as well, increased sales, maybe not to the level enjoyed because of Free Trade access, but some sales nevertheless. With the tariff imposed being paid by both the consumer and manufacturer, it is a win win situation with either purchase.

By following the Plaza Accord and Garten's suggestions, the policy makers created a disaster. After reaching a peak in value in March 1985, the dollar lost 30.4% of its value by the end of the decade. In the 90's, the dollar's value was level or below the value enjoyed during the mid 1970's. It did strengthen lightly in the late 90's due mainly because of three financial world wide crises: The Mexican crisis in 1995 when the Pesos collapsed in value against the dollar, the Asian crisis of 1997 touched off by the Barings Bank fiasco, and Japan's recession in 1998. It was not because of the Plaza Accord as the Globalist would like everyone to believe.

What Baker didn't realize was that four prior attempts to solve the balance of payments by devaluation did not work? Why doesn't Garten, a man who lived through these 4 devaluations suggest more of this horrendous policy? He is either ignorant, which is unlikely, or he is "one of them" Globalist. As citizens, one cannot sit back and examine this man's experience and take his suggestions for granted. What worked for years under protectionism was the economics of scale kept prices down, not imports. As Alexander Hamilton predicted correctly many years ago that it was domestic competition that brings prices down, not imports.

Patrick Buchanan wrote an article in IBD Nov. 24, 2008 outlining the unfair practices the Asian car manufactures have enjoyed at the cost to the US manufacturers. Because the Asian manufacturers did not have to abide by the health and safety standards imposed by our federal regulations, they did not incur those extra costs. Because Asian manufacturers did not have corporate tax rates, local rates, property rates and sales taxes, like the US manufacturers had to pay, the Asian car companies enjoyed more savings. How can Free Trade be called free, when the US imports 700,000 cars from South Korea while they import only 5,000 cars from the US? A recent solution is to force the US labor Unions to accept lower wages, comparable to the non union workers employed by foreign car companies working in the US. Isn't this lowering our standards to meet the competitions? Why don't we go to the World Trade Organization and seek laws for foreign automakers to raise their safety and health standards to our levels. Wouldn't this seem practical, we are raising the bar to excellence? I have never heard of lowering the bar to mediocrity!! Would an appeal to the WTO work? Does this lowering of standards resemble the leveling of the seesaw I mentioned, and play into the objectives of the WTO and globalism/socialism? Will we be better off in the next few years than we were in the 1950's, 60's, 80's? For the first time, in US history, manufacturing employs fewer workers than the government, and doesn't this seem like socialism?!! In fact, the number of state and federal employees is growing and sustaining these positions by taxing a shrinking private workforce spells gloom.

Legal Impact

Article Six of the General Agreement on Tariffs and Trade, GATT, and the predecessor of the World Trade Organization, WTO sets rules prohibiting dumping. However, through dumping practices, big multinationals cripple the indigenous food companies of developing countries before they can get off the ground. They stifle competition before it gets to big to handle, and WTO rules make it difficult for the small indigenous companies to prove harm to the sector involved. It also promotes the dependency on these foreign multinational food companies.

"Dumping is one of the most damaging of all current distortions in world trade practices," according to Kristen Dawkins, Vice President of Global Programs at the Institute for Agriculture and Trade Policy. Developing country's agriculture, vital for food security, livelihoods, poverty reduction and trade are being crippled by major food companies who dump their commodities into these countries below the local prices. In essence, the local people cannot sell their commodities, and make a living. These big Wal Mart types, through the economy of scale are putting the mom and pop shops out of business.

Examples of stronger powers enacted by the WTO include the non tariff arenas of environment, health, and workers rights, which, while somewhat altruistic yet controversial towards social goals, can be seen as an obstacle to world trade. One sweeping revision made through the years of GATT Rounds, (Rounds are terms for multi year meetings, one may remember the Uruguay Rounds of 1994) and later made part of the WTO is "most favored nation" status. This status is a principle that if a country grants a certain privilege to one country, it must grant the same privilege to all GATT member countries. Another broad and destructive policy of the WTO is "National Treatment," which states that a nation is required to give equal treatment to foreign imports of goods and services as to domestic goods and services. This essentially allows the WTO to place downward pressure on each nation's laws to match a lower standard devised by the WTO. Thus, if the US Congress passes a law for certain health and environmental standards for a certain industry, a country with lower standards could file a complaint with the WTO that the standards for the US are too restrictive and are an impediment to trade. The WTO can then overrule the US Congress and force the US to lower its standards so other nations have access to the US markets. Has this happened? Yes! Despite the US laws on human rights, and child labor, other nations simply don't abide by these US standards. On environmental causes, the Tuna outcry a few years back caused a stir. The US law banned all Tuna from nations that used nets which caught Tuna and trapped and then killed dolphins. Do you need reminders about the tomato disease, mad cow epidemic, Chinese toys? The WTO disallows the enforcement of US laws, so any proponent of "save the animals" is befuddled. Therefore, the WTO, this ban of unelected and unknown bureaucrats, has acquired global authority over all nations. It has undermined the pillars of democracy, the practice of citizens to elect public officials and make laws that protect and serve the citizenry of each nation and promote the general welfare of nations.

One of the most controversial and damaging policy initiatives that came out of the Uruguay Round was stronger enforcement mechanisms in the WTO. For example, if one nation files a formal complaint with the WTO that some other nation's laws or trade regulations, while being beneficial to that country, is protectionist and against the WTO's trade rules, that country can file a lawsuit. In turn, the WTO, can rule that the nation comply with the WTO standards. And if said nation fails to comply, can allow the complainant nation to impose trade sanctions.

Example. In a Nov. 26 2004 article in the NY Times, the WTO was expected to approve the imposition of $150 million in trade sanctions against the US by the European Union, Japan, Canada, and four other nations in response to the Byrd anti dumping law. With trade surpluses enjoyed by all these complainants, this excessive greed is sickening. The Byrd law states that anti dumping tariffs (a fee or surcharge foreign companies pay for access to US consumer markets, much like the tariffs of old that were paid directly to the US Treasury) collected on cheap foreign imports be paid to the competitive domestic companies. The suits claims the tariffs punished importers twice; once with the tariff payment and secondly distributing the money directly to the companies, competitors of the importers. Byrd had it half right. The tariff was a good idea; it protected domestic manufacturer while simultaneously generating revenue. Where Byrd was wrong was with the distribution to the companies; the money should have flowed into either the state or federal treasury. This is the money previously mentioned that the Federal Government used for Federal expenditures rather than taxing its' citizens. How can these countries still complain when they all enjoy a trade surplus at the expense of our jobs, our dollar's decline, and higher taxes?

Two more recent examples of the WTO reigning authority of US laws appeared on the front page in the April 18th 2004 edition of The New York Times, "NAFTA Tribunals Stir US Worries." In the article, Chief Justice Margaret Marshall of the Massachusetts court heard at a dinner party that her earlier ruling would be subject to review by an international tribunal. The second case reveals the tribunal's authority over US laws by declaring a Mississippi law is at odds with international law leaving the US liable for millions of dollars in damages. This international body with assumed or self granted authority is overruling a US law. This phantom body supersedes our domestic laws. That's right, if the International Tribunal of the WTO rules against the Mississippi family, US tax dollars would have to pay the million dollar fines.

In the article, counting Chief Justice Marshall, two lawyers, three judges, one being the plaintiff's lawyer, and one Presidential candidate, John Kerry, stated their surprise and concern over the Tribunal's authority over US laws. Two Law Professors, Georgetown's John D. Echeverria commented that this is the biggest threat to United States judicial independence that no one has heard of and even fewer people understand. The other law Professor, Hofstra's Peter Spiro points to: "the fundamental reorientation of our constitutional system. You have an international tribunal essentially reviewing American court judgments." Beside Chief justice Marshall, Chief Justice Ronald M. George of the California Supreme Court remarked: "It's rather shocking that the high courts of the state and federal governments could have their judgments circumvented by these tribunals."

Former Chief Judge of the Federal Appeals Court in Washington and one of the three judges who sat on the tribunal for the Mississippi case and who of course declined to discuss the ruling, but did add, " If Congress had known anything about this in NAFTA, they would never have voted for it. The other two judges filling out the tribunal are from Australia and Britain, selected by the parties from a panel and whose rulings cannot be appealed. They can appeal US law, but not WTO law. Who selected these people to the panel?

Senator John Kerry said nothing was discussed about this provision of tribunals, as outlined in Chapter 11 of NAFTA, because no one knew how it would play out. The lawyer for the plaintiff, John H. Lewis, "Agreed with the principle that people should not short circuit or second guess the American legal system."

Can one imagine how all this happened? Congress, under financial incentives from lobbyists, and under pressure from big business, all directed by Globalists, and because of the bi-partisanship of the bill, passed NAFTA without thoroughly reviewing any potentially and damaging means by which foreigners can use to dismantle our sovereignty. NAFTA did not come up for deliberations in committees, as stipulated in the Constitution; it was "Fast Tracked" with an up or down vote and no one checked the fine print!! Congress received their illicit cash, voting favors and deals brokered, and no one checked to see if anyone locked the doors.

Another area where NAFTA has failed is the secret provision in the agreement for tribunals to impose financial damages and impose undue regulations on the United States. Under NAFTA, any foreign country or company may sue for damages and dismantle or disregard environmental, health and safety regulations in our country. To date, lawsuits and claims of $13 billion dollars have been filed against US companies. How does this work?

One example is the banana fight in South America that affected Europe and then affected the United States. Domestic banana companies were sued by a South American country and the US imposed a tariff and restrictions to our markets. Being a French Colony, they appealed to France which imposed limitations on US goods being shipped into France and also withholding their exporting any luxury items, wine and cheese and Louis Vuitton luggage come to mind. Any lawsuit filed for any unjustifiable means, is heard by the World Trade Organization or WTO. This unelected group can then decide against the US and dismantle or allow these companies not to abide by any environmental, health, or safety laws enacted by our elected officials. Think of this. Some banana grower in South America can change the laws in this country by going over our legislatures' heads and appealing to the WTO to change all the laws passed by the US Congress that are supposed to ensure safety, health and environmental concerns.

In summary, the Globalists have achieved all of their goals. With the WTO and the Trade Experts that continue to promote and perpetuate their socialist goals, the Globalist has in place the mechanisms to continue their socialization through all continents. Just like the European Union, the Free Trade Agreement of the Americas is next, where I am sure the Globalist will promote an "American" currency, much like the Euro. This will consolidate Canada, the United States and Mexico with South America into one entity. Free Trade of the Pacific is another form of work in progress. In essence, the Globalist is working towards consolidating the nations into three regions, European, Americas, and Asian where control and manipulation of three Globalist-made entities will be easier to manage and socialize than 270 separate nations.

It would be great if more people were aware of this, asked their congressmen about it and question local officials, the media and expose citizens to what has been happening to the sovereignty of the US. It would then be necessary to find the method to restore the tariff and trade regulations back to the Legislative Branch and not some world governing body of unelected officials deciding how to run our country.

Why all this? Remember, controlling a country's currency expedites the advent of socialism. Now, imagine a see-saw as an example with the US up high on one side and Europe on the other down low. This is historically accurate. Since all this began in 1913, the see-saw is balancing itself. Through their Trade, Taxation and Federal Reserve manipulations the Globalists have dismantled the US side, thus lowering it while simultaneously raising the European side in order to strike a balance. Achievement! How? The revaluation of currencies and the subjection of dismantling sovereign nation's currencies into the European currency is one. Secondly, the passage of the Free Trade Act of the Americas or FTAA meant to copy the procedures as happened in Europe. North America will become a Trade Zone, much like Europe and eventually a one dollar currency most likely US dollar will be the currency for this hemisphere. Lastly, with work being done on the Free Trade of the Pacific, and the current revaluation suggested by Garten, expect a Trade Zone of the Pacific, with its own currency. The conclusion is the Globalists will have achieved their goal. They will have reduced the number of currencies down to three to make their manipulations easier.

With the European Union struggling to define itself as a political and economic entity, member countries are becoming skeptical about the Union's constitution taking effect in 2007. Using the United States as a model, the European community is already calling itself the United States of Europe. Member countries do not like the EU's constitution, which strips sovereignty from national governments, creates oppressive new social rules and places the entire community under control of bureaucrats in Brussels and Luxembourg. In short, the constitution is a 270 page "socialist" nightmare.

In a recent speech at Georgetown University, Justice Sandra Day O'Connor praised the role of international law commenting: "International law is no longer a specialty if judges are going to faithfully discharge their duties." She has further professed that foreign legal opinions may not only enrich our own countries decision, it may create a good impression.

Justice Kennedy has cited rulings from a British parliamentary vote and from a European Court of Human Rights. Justice Breyer referred to decisions found in the Privy Council of Jamaica, and the Supreme Court of India and Zimbabwe. Have the Globalist influenced some of our Justices? Are these Justices making these comments to condition the public to get accustomed to hearing these statements of using foreign courts to overrule our laws? Thankfully, the US has Justice Scalia supporting the US constitution when he maintained the Supreme Court should not impose foreign moods, fads or fashions on Americans.

The WTO or World Trade Organization was ratified by President Clinton in 1994. It passed through both houses relatively easily. What is wrong is that Clinton went against the constitution and signed it before Congress deliberated; a constitutional procedure first ignored and then allowed. The dismantling began n 1909 with the Payne Aldrich tariff Act followed by the passage post World War II of stronger provisions in the Treaty of 1934, changing the term "Treaty" to "Agreements" enabling the President to bypass even further the US Constitution. The US essentially agreed to a higher authority, the WTO, whose rulings and decisions supersede the US Constitution. If the US disagrees with a WTO ruling, a decision arrived at behind closed doors, (like the Fed. Reserve meetings) where an insignificant country like

Ghana could impose a ruling and the WTO would then impose sanctions and penalties on the US.

Who runs the WTO? No one knows. These emissaries aren't even elected, they are appointed and by whom? They tend to be wealthy individuals or associates of wealthy people. Why; because the extremely wealthy have the most to gain from controlling global trade.

The WTO basically is a global alliance similar to the United Nations for politics, between Globalists who have usurped global trade regulations from the individual nations and transferred the regulation of trade to their own domicile. These unelected and unknown officials have destroyed the sovereignty of nations in their effort to socialize the world. Their history of eschewing human rights concerns, environmental laws and labor standards of individual countries is done for the bottom line; to make themselves richer regardless of the impact of their decisions.

Post Civil War, trade deficits shrank until it became a positive number or trade surplus by 1880, and remained in positive territory for almost 100 years until 1971. Except for two years during the recession of 1991 and 1992, in which the trade deficit still remained negative, it slowly increased until the passage of NAFTA went into effect in 1994. NAFTA's first year shows a deficit jump of $55 billion dollars from the previous year. It has since climbed to over $400 billion dollars. And why is NAFTA good for America? Why do we as a country want more of this bad medicine? Doesn't this go against what Hamilton learned from Postlethwayt? What has this done to the value of the dollar?

Now one can see how the Globalist have taken a

country with no debt, no taxes, and the highest standard of living and has slowly eroded the preeminence of the United States, where this country is running huge trade and fiscal debts, has imposed confiscatory taxation all in the name of Free Trade. Free Trade and the trade imbalances weakened the value of the US dollar, which necessitates a duel income family and exasperates the general standard of living. Through their destructive trade policies, the Globalists are achieving a Socialist world.

TAXES

How did the United States travel from a world where it had no national debt, no taxes and the highest standard of living in early 1900's to a world in which there are now numerous forms of taxes at variable rates and $5 trillion (and counting) in debt in 100 years?

How did the United States politicians arrive at taxation? What was their purpose? Why and how do these taxes keep reaching higher levels, and why and how do they ever expand into other areas for consumers, like sin taxes, gasoline taxes, death, conveyance taxes etc? It is all very explainable.

In essence, taxes exist for several reasons. The first reason is to offset lost revenues from bad trade and monetary policy and wars. Using the result of progressive taxation, "redistribution of wealth" the second reason is to create a socialistic country by creating two classes. One "ruling" class will exist for the wealthy. The lower class will exist to work for the upper wealthy class, in this case, the Globalists. Through excessive taxation, a working class will find it more difficult to escape poverty and become self reliant, thereby creating more government dependency. This is exactly what the ruling class wants. They want to install the means to perpetuate their workforce. By creating more forms of taxes, they want the masses to shift from self reliance to government dependency for education, shelter, health care, jobs, subsistence etc.

The second reason for taxation is to spread democracy

and freedom throughout the world which is expensive. In conjunction, once a free democracy is established, Globalists can introduce a socialistic agenda to encompass the country into the One World fold of the Globalists. Free trade policies that have shifted US industrial and manufacturing jobs overseas and the outsourcing of technology jobs both have contributed to the effort to foster democracy at the expense of huge job losses and a shrinking tax base. Using tax dollars, the US government, through the World Bank, The Import-Export Bank to name a few, have spread capitalism/democracy to third world countries at the expense of the US citizen. While this investment fosters growth, what happens to the US geopolitically? Does it cause a shrinking middle class? Perhaps! Does it make it harder for taxpayers to earn a good living, find a good job with hope for a future? Most certainly. Does it level the playing field, the seesaw example where the third world countries side rises, and the US side lowers, thereby eroding the standard of living? Yes. However it is the excessive taxation which is paying for it all. With post WWII Free Trade policies enacted, allowing for Japan and Germany to develop electronics and automobile businesses which has enabled them to embrace democracy, but at what price to the US citizen. When does assistance become too much sacrifice? Spreading dollars in third world countries to bolster their economy and standard of living at the cost of US taxpayers is getting too expensive. Does the US commit too much money to foreign countries so that future wars grown from the "Seed Money" invested by the US become too much to walk away from and the military is used to protect the investment? Do these humanitarian efforts eventually produce a diplomatic concern or eventually a costly war?

For an historical perspective, no taxes existed until the Stamp Act imposed on the US by Great Britain, and everyone knows the Boston Tea Party and the American Revolution followed. During the writing of the Constitution, Hamilton knew taxation was an anathema to the citizens. He had tried a direct taxation on distilled spirits and people in western Pennsylvania revolted in what became known as the Whiskey Rebellion in 1794. Where is our out cry today against all kinds of direct taxation?

With a few exceptions of some sort of temporary taxes, be it a war tax or inheritance tax, installed for emergency purposes like a tax during the Civil War, which destroyed the economy as described in Trade, taxes did not exist. Tariffs supplied the revenues for government expenditures. Working citizens kept all of there hard earned money. Imagine that today. In CT., citizens work 160 days a year JUST to pay the taxes.

Jack Kemp cited in The Investors Business Daily, President Lincoln once remarked in his acceptance speech , "I don't believe in a law to prevent a man from getting rich; it would do more harm than good." This sentiment is applicable today.

Returning to the theory of socializing this country, control over the money supply began with the passage of The Federal Reserve Act in 1913, forming of the Federal Reserve System, and the legality of instituting a federal income tax. Now with taxation reaching and continuing to reach into the pocketbooks and wallets of the citizenry, the Globalists are making significant steps towards their goal. With reduced tariffs lowering the revenue for the treasury, taxation mythically arrived as the sole solution to make up for the shortfall. Taxation was also designed to redistribute the wealth; another Globalist design to introduce socialism. Why? With taxation, the government could legally steal hard earned dollars and spread their socialistic agenda while simultaneously and gradually decreasing the self sufficiency of the citizenry and shift dependency to the government.

As previously mentioned, it was the protective tariffs which funded the US government for 125 years, up through the McKinley presidency. During McKinley's term, the US enjoyed a federal surplus, low unemployment, the world's highest standard of living and no Income Tax. The US did not need an Income Tax because the monies generated by these tariffs covered the expenses of the US government. Doesn't anyone remember the term "The Roaring 90's?" As mentioned in William Gill's "Trade Wars Against America," it was the Payne-Aldrich Tariff Act of 1909 which slashed the tariffs, thereby decreasing the amount of money flowing into the Treasury. Shortly thereafter, in 1913, to make up the shortfall in funds, the government passed the 16th Amendment creating the Income Tax.

How? A harbinger of things to come, a fateful event was the Spanish American War in 1898. Nothing like a war to create the "chaos" or a "Rothschild Job" required altering the life of the citizenry. Controversial evidence and suspicion as to the real cause of the battleship Maine's explosion is still debated. Nonetheless, because of the war, custom revenues were down, so a 15% Inheritance Tax was imposed to assist paying for the war. Post war, in 1902, this inheritance tax was repealed. A few years earlier, in 1900, Congress, with McKinley's approval, passed the Currency Act placing the US on the gold standard and ensuring the treasury department maintained parity between the dollar and gold. (40) McKinley's objective of a sound economic policy remained intact.

However, with the war's conclusion, and repeal of the tax, general prosperity and welfare throughout the nation returned. So the Globalist realized that their socialist goal of world government and control of the money supply was slowly losing momentum. Something had to be done to restore their socialistic plan and implement the means to do so: their emphasis on slashing the tariffs, forming a central bank, and instituting the income tax. The Globalist knew that McKinley and his protective measures had to go and have him replaced by a surrogate member.

The Globalists did this by arranging for the assassination of President McKinley in 1902. Enter Theodore Roosevelt. McKinley was shot in 1901, Garfield in 1881, and Lincoln in 1865. All three were strong supporters of protectionism. Coincidence? I think not. Roosevelt expanded the government, and with expansion comes expenses. The war reparations brought Cuba, Puerto Rico, Guam and the Philippines under US control; lands which could be used to spread democracy, US influence, wealth, power etc., which necessitated expenditures to manage. (41) Roosevelt had the Navy build the Great White Fleet, and instructed the Army to take over construction of the Panama Canal. In 1903, the US received authority to construct a naval base on Cuba. However, the expenses grew faster than the revenue stream from custom duties. By 1908, realizing the costs of this expansion, Roosevelt needed more funds, but where? The added decline in revenue brought by the tariff reductions exasperated the shrinking revenue stream.

Globalist's concocted a scheme. Creating the concept of sensing suspicions about tariffs creating monopolies, they ordered a tariff review. While Roosevelt lowered tariffs, which even provided less money for his expensive and expansive government programs, he attempted to usher in a graduated income tax. However, years before, the US Supreme Court ruled that an **Income Tax was unconstitutional**, so the Globalists re-phrased it as an "excise tax."

By 1909, Taft replaced Roosevelt as President. It was during this transition that a heated debate on tariffs was brewing in Congress. The debate led by Cordell Hull of Tennessee wasn't so much about the tariffs as it was about the graduated income tax mulled over as the means to replace the shortfall in revenues from previous tariff reductions. Strange to think congressmen didn't debate returning to the means that worked for so long in generating government revenue, tariffs. While individual states were debating with this constitutional amendment, President Taft proposed an income tax on corporations in the meantime until the states returned with a decision. Taft renamed the levy an "excise" tax because of the Supreme Court ruling. With the passage of the Payne Aldrich Tariff Act of 1909, a provision included in the document was the constitutional amendment to "authorize" a graduated income tax. By 1913, the income tax became a reality, levying a tax at 1% of $3,000.00 for incomes of single filers and 1% of $4,000.00 for married couples. (42) Today, these rates are considerably higher, yet back then there were no other forms of taxes, e.g. capital gains, inheritance etc.

Returning to the theory of socializing this country, control over the money supply began with the Federal Reserve System in 1913, and the socialistic induced income tax which began reaching and has continued to reach into the pocketbooks and wallets of the citizenry. The plan's secondary intention is using the destructive trade and monetary policy to force layoffs transferring jobs overseas and fostering their government dependency initiative. With reduced tariffs lowering the revenue for the treasury, taxation arrived to make up for the short-fall. The Globalists shifted the burden of generating revenues from foreign countries to US citizens. Does this seem appropriate? Taxation was also designed to redistribute the wealth; another Globalist design to introduce socialism.

At the outbreak of World War I, the United States was literally an industrial juggernaut; having nearly 36 percent of the world's total industrial output, far more than any other two countries combined. Germany and Great Britain placed second and third with 16 percent and 15 percent respectively. Despite France's and Russia's vast natural resources they combined for under 12 percent. So, one gets a clear picture of the enormity and power of the US economy. However, just prior to the war, in 1914, the economy suffered mightily. The Underwood Tariff of 1913 which reduced tariffs even further, combined with the Federal Reserve, had sent the nation's industrial leaders into a panic. The Bradstreet Journal reported the largest number of business failures than ever previously recorded. Andrew Carnegie wrote President

Wilson describing he has never seen conditions like this for debtors to pay. Financial conditions were so horrendous, that by July, the New York Stock Exchange, which kept its' doors open during the 1907 panic, did in fact close its doors. Where was Mr. Morgan this time? Why and how did the Federal Reserve, designed to prevent such disasters allow this to happen in its' first year of existence? This is the financial chaos I like to mention the globalists use to further their socialist goals.

As previously mentioned, it is known early in the 20th century US citizens enjoyed the highest standard of living. To review, from 1901 and McKinely's presidency, when prosperity prevailed without a federal debt, without taxation and a Federal Reserve System to 1920 and post war America, a 20 year span, the Globalists achieved multiple goals. They created a financial chaos which led to the Federal Reserve. They achieved financial and economic ruin and implemented taxation, the confiscatory means for revenue generation, displacing the tried and true practice of tariffs. They ensnarled the US into foreign war, creating a $25 billion debt further exasperating the financial situation and legitimizing the taxes to pursue their socialistic goals. President McKinley's assassination occurred in 1901, followed by the Panic of 1907, the Underwood Tariff followed by The Federal Reserve Act and with it the Income Tax in 1913. In a dozen short years, the Globalists reversed the financially sound US economic system without taxation into a debt ridden inflationary prone economically disastrous one. This follows the "Chaos"formula I believe the Socialists use to introduce their sinister plans.

The financial ramifications of World War I were

dramatic. The national debt of $1.2 billion in 1916 swelled to over $25 billion by the end of the war. On a per capita basis, the debt rose from $12 per person to $242. The economic situation worsened with the Federal Reserve raising the re-discount rate from 4 to 7 percent and the post war recession began in the summer of 1920. However, Globalist's goals to introduce the League of Nations for world government failed. Their secondary desire for socialistic goals, taxation, fostered by the creation of the war debt also lost steam thanks mainly to the Secretary of Treasury Mellon.

What succeeded in extricating the US economy from the recession was the passage of the Fordney-McCumber Tariff Act of 1922. This undid the disastrous effects of the Underwood Tariff of 1913 which prompted the business failures and Carnegie's letter to Wilson. The duties on iron ore and steel, which had been eliminated in 1913, were restored. The tariffs on sugar, wool and textiles were all increased. With the enactment of the tariff, an economic resurgence followed. Enhancing the prosperity, Andrew Mellon, Secretary of the Treasury, lowered taxes. Combining the tax cuts which spurred growth, and with an increase in custom duties, Mellon achieved budget surplus year after year and reduced the war debt by almost a third by the end of the decade. The "Gatsby" era of the Roaring 20's resulted.

By the late 1920's, sensing a return to more prosperous times and realizing a potential derailment of their goals, the Globalists needed another "chaos" to get the country back on the socialistic track. So, they orchestrated the Crash of 1929.

The Stock Market Crash of 1929 was not brought on

by the Smoot Hawley Tariff as every text book, economist suggests. The tariff was enacted eight months after
the crash, so how could it be responsible? The Globalists
want everyone to believe it, because by placing blame on
tariffs, the tried and rue practice, it will never be offered
as a viable solution to economic woes. This is exactly what
they want. What occurred was simply a blowing up of a
bubble and then popping it as orchestrated by these Globalists. Post WWI, Great Britain's economy inflated more
than the US. To create parity between the two countries,
Britain convinced the US to inflate its economy. The Governor of the Federal Reserve System, Benjamin Strong
and the Governor of the Bank of England, Montagu
Norman, conspired together and convinced Secretary of
the Treasury Andrew Mellon to implement two monetary
policies. One was to monetize the Fed, which he did by
about $2 billion dollars by 1927 along with reducing the
discount rate from 4 to 3.5 percent. (32) Both initiatives
allowed commercial banks to loan more dollars. Between
1924-1929, the Federal Reserve created and infused the
economy with about $11 billion "fiat" dollars. All that
was needed now was to pop this expanding bubble. The
Federal Reserve accomplished this in August of 1929 by
raising the discount rate to 6 percent and simultaneously
selling securities in the open market. Both policies shrank
the money supply and tightened credit and the Crash
of 29 ensued. Here is another example of how the Federal Reserve manipulates the monetary policy at will and
against the wishes of elected officials. It is also another
example to criticize the Fed and ask how and why this
happened when the design of the Fed was to prevent
this from happening again. This is very similar to Alan

Greenspan manipulation of the monetary policy when he blew up the bubble in the late 1990's which allowed for the Crash which began in the summer of 2000. Is the Housing Crisis of 2007-2008 similar? Yes, more on this in Final Thoughts.

An attempt for world government, as previously mentioned as one of Rhodes' objectives, appeared through World War I. Taxes were negligible in the 1920's, but with the depression and World War II, the Globalist took a huge leap towards socialization. How? The Depression gave the powers-that-be the chance to transfer control from the individual to the government; to President Roosevelt and his social programs. Self reliance went out the window and government dependence came through the door. More and more people relied on the government for basic necessities: food, clothing, jobs, shelter etc

Prior to this more people enjoyed the fruits of their labor and kept more of their hard earned money and they could afford these basic necessities and the "wants" or luxuries which further propel the economy. Now, the depression changed the attitude of the populace. The government's condescending attitude meant it could look down on the people and say I control you, you need me for everything and since you depend on me, I will tell you how things should be run. I will tell you how to work, how long to work, and how much you pay me, the government, in taxes. The tides have turned. Where once people gave the government a "budget" and were told to operate the government, now the government is telling the citizenry how much the government wants, not needs, and bills the taxpayer. The tax paying citizens have become the slaves to the government.

When expenses continue to rise higher than income, the government introduces more and progressive taxes to feed their spending appetite. This vicious cycle continues until more people become unemployed, due to poor fiscal and monetary policy, thereby forcing the government to tax the dwindling number of remaining people in the workforce to assist the unemployed. The numbers get inverted: Where once more people worked and paid less in taxes to the present day where fewer numbers of people are working yet are paying more in taxes. This is because of an increase in the number of people who become dependent on the government for subsistence. Ever hear about the ever widening income gap, the growing gap between the "haves" and the "have nots?" This is their form socialism at work, creating a wealthy ruling class and a poor subservient lower class that works for the ruling class and not themselves. It sounds very similar to Russian peasants working for Mother Russia. Is this the "merging" mentioned by Gather?

Back to post World War II where another opportunity for the Globalists to seize control presents itself. By amassing huge debts, the government could use the war as an excuse to tax and increase taxes even higher to pay off the war debt. This seemed justified by the people, and they paid, but unlike previous war reparations when taxes stopped after paying off the debt, this tax continued. The government again was not going to shut off this flow of money. So now you have in the course of forty years, the change in the public's attitude of relenting to paying a marginal tax, to consenting to pay a tax.

One other example of Federal Reserve meddling occurred during Truman's presidency. With high taxes, offset by the still high purchasing power of the dollar, and non defense spending reductions, the federal deficit remained relatively low, less than $18 billion for the three years of the Korean War. High individual taxes were generated because returning World War II soldiers were flush with money and wanted to be productive. The post war economy flourished with new technologies, TV's, radios, and the automobile, items once just for the wealthy, were now affordable for the middle class.

The public accepted the tax increase to pay the war expenses; it was the patriotic thing to do!! However, the public grew accustomed to it and the government was hush hush about dismantling it after paying little of the war debt. (33) Why turn off this cash cow?

More of the Globalist's selective memory follows when they fail to mention lower taxes under a democratic Kennedy that provided for economic expansion. Did the Globalists purposely omit JFK's success because his prescription to revive an economy is something they are against; across the board tax cuts? During the debate on President Bush's tax cuts soon after his 2000 election, doesn't everyone remember the conservative talk shows reciting the old recordings of JFK promoting lowering taxes to expand the economy, thus providing for new companies, new jobs? I remember.

In an article about cutting taxes, Mr. Kemp argues for cutting taxes by citing a President Kennedy speech in 1960. According to Kemp, Kennedy remarked: "It is increasingly clear that no matter what party is in power, so long as our national security needs keep rising, an economy hampered by restrictive tax rates will never produce enough revenues to balance our budget, just as it will never produce enough jobs or enough profits. Surely, the lesson of the last decade is that deficits are not caused by wild eyed spenders, but by slow economic growth and periodic recessions and any new recession will break all deficit records." As further evidence of Kennedy's tax cuts pledge, he remarked in 1962: "It is a paradoxical truth that tax rates are too high and tax revenues are too low, and the soundest way to raise revenue in the long run is to cut taxes now."

Johnson and his "Great Society" emerged spending huge amounts on socialistic programs. There was, and still is a "War on Poverty" that has cost $5 trillion dollars and counting. One would think that after forty years and $5 trillion dollars, the problem would be close to being solved.

In the early 1970's Nixon was forced to remove the US off the gold standard. Here is one example where trade policy is linked to tax policy. As a result of the first trade deficit in the early 1970's when the value of the dollar began its descent, higher interest rates were needed by Carter's years to attract foreign investments to cover expenses. By floating fiat dollars throughout the world, the gold reserves in Fort Knox could not cover the inflationary practices of printing more money. Too many "fiat" dollars could be redeemed for the gold in Fort Knox and could have wiped the US clean. Remember the inflation definition, too many dollars chasing too few goods, which is exactly what happened. Interest Rates were raised to 21% to attract foreign investors. How does that rate compare in today's world of 5-6 %? Inflation rates increased to double digit levels and recession followed.

Because of a trade deficit, (think of Postlywait and Hamilton) a decline in value of the dollar forces the requirement for more money and taxes go up. Further assistance from increases in tax revenues were needed and tax rates rose up to 70% for the top bracket by the late 1970's. Doesn't anyone remember the "wonderful" economy during Carter's presidency? Was removing the US from the Gold standard an intentional Globalist plot? One could assume so. Was it done to level the seesaw with the rest of the world with regard to standard of living? Perhaps. Wasn't the Federal Reserve designed to prevent these up and down cycles? Was the 70's crisis a form of "chaos" the Globalist use to implement their socialist agenda?

Enter President Ronald Reagan. After entering office and inheriting a terrible economy and lack of confidence in the American Dream, Reagan pushed for and got his tax cuts. His idea of Supply Side economics works. It worked in the 1920's, under Secretary Mellon, under President Kennedy in the 1960's, and in the 1980's under President Reagan. Critics like to state his supply side policies caused the biggest deficit in history. However, much of his deficit spending was applied to the military establishment which provided two positive effects. It hired workers which in turn paid taxes, but most importantly, the defense spending help win the cold war, both positive outcomes.

Another example of tax reduction having a positive impact is when Reagan changed the murky investment climate into a one where investments receive rewards. To revive an economy, investors need to invest and will only do so when an attractive investment climate arises. Investors need an incentive to invest; if too much of their profits are taken by taxes they won't invest. For example, prior to 1979, when Long Term Capital Gains taxes were 35%, the IPO market averaged 30 new start-ups a year.

From 1979-1982 thanks to Reagan when that tax rate was cut significantly to 20%, investments poured in. In that first year of 1982, under the 20% incentive there were 681 IPO's. (44) This translates into new companies, new products, new and more jobs, and more taxpayers which foster higher tax revenues. Mellon did this in the 1920's. Kennedy accomplished this in the 1960's. Some of the companies from the 1980's are Home Depot, Microsoft, Oracle, Dell, Cisco and American Online. Think of the number of employees from these companies receiving paychecks, spending, saving, investing and enlarging the tax base of communities. Think of where this country is with regard to Global leadership because of the tax break incentive for investors to invest in these companies. Think of the technology society enjoys because of these companies. Now think where this country might have been without these tax breaks which inspired investments in these start ups. With Bush's tax breaks, just think of the next Home Depots and Microsoft's. Doesn't it make sense to have tax breaks to provide the companies and job growth of tomorrow? Bush wants this. Without this tax incentive, investors for new start-ups sit on the sideline, stagnation follows and recession results.

In his article which appeared in Investor's Business Dailey on August 10th 2001, Jack Kemp revealed some interesting and provocative examples of how intrusive, expensive and economically destructive taxes can be. Mr. Kemp revealed how when President Ronald Reagan lowered the marginal tax rate from 50 to 28 percent but increased the capital gains to 28%, treating it like ordinary income, the capital gains tax revenue fell from $165 billion in 1985 to $116 billion in 1992. Remember when

Bush 1 inherited a bad economy and was forced to "Read my lips" and raise taxes. He lost the election!

On a smaller scale using CT as an example of the national problem before 1991, CT did not have a state income tax or the $300 million in casino revenue generated by a 25% tax on slots, and the state managed. CT. had the highest sales tax in the nation to generate revenue. Tough times in the late 1980's prompted discussion of an income tax. The income tax combined with the elimination of the sales tax was supposed to be a temporary fix and then removed; like the "temporary war tax" of the late 1940's. However, the state income tax remains, as does the sales tax and new forms of taxation are still under discussion, namely sin taxes and a millionaire's tax. A new "Conveyance Tax" was imposed, designed to tax the proceeds from the sale of a home. This is in addition to the Capital Gains Tax realized on the sale as well!!!! What has been the taxes effect on CT's economy and overall welfare? How did CT survive before all these forms of taxes and Casino Revenue?

By 1993, shortly after the state income tax started its effect, the state's budget was $8.08 billion dollars and in June 2004, just 10 years later, the General Assembly passed a $13.2 billion dollar budget. (45) This $5 billion dollar increase in 10 years calculates approximately to a 6% raise in spending each year for 10 consecutive years. Will any private sector salaried taxpayer who received a 6% raise in pay each year for the last 10 years please stand up! Put another way, the democratic controlled General Assembly spent an extra $500 million dollars each year for 10 consecutive years. And they wonder why they are called the tax and spend party? What has happened to all the money? What is there to show for all the spending? Public education (UConn exception) in many areas is in decline, poverty and homelessness remains, transportation is still in disarray, and no financially sound economic development to replace the state's income tax as the sole means to generate revenue seems to be in place to generate and sustain these expenses. Yet, despite the income tax, the casino revenue, the state is over a billion in debt. Why? How? Where has the money gone? With the huge and unreliable stock market induced tax revenues of the late 90's, the General Assembly unwisely overspent. What did the state spend money on that before 1991 was not needed? The money was spent on the growing number of individuals dependent on the government. Why are they dependent? They are dependent because of fiscally unsound economic policies. Excessive taxation forces companies and workers to leave the state eroding the corporate and sales base further. For CT residents, think of the Hartford Whalers departure. The aforementioned free trade policies contribute to the decline in workforce shrinking the already diminishing tax base. Now with years of market decline, the tax revenues aren't there to cover these unknown expenses. Increase in taxes is not the answer. A review of where unnecessary spending occurs is needed and should be curtailed.

For an example of market declines, in the upper income echelon of people with more than $10 million dollars, their income declined by 63% and the total capital gains revenue fell 29%. All these tax revenues which support federal, state and local expenditures declined and a budget deficit resulted. No wonder.

Statistics reveal that 12% of the people that made

over $200,000 dollars slipped to under that level by 2002. (46) Hence the budgets derived during an economic boom could not be sustained during a drop in overall tax revenue collection. Kennedy was right. Reagan was right. A state or federal budget cannot be sustained on future tax revenues based on fluctuating consumer usage, be it gas tax revenue, casino revenue etc.

Between 2000-2002 middle class incomes increased nearly 5% according to IRS statistics, whereas overall individual income declined 5% during this same period because the top tax bracket lost 28% of income on average from the stock crash, portfolio decline and a decline in the number of high paying jobs being outsourced in the free trade name of competitiveness.

Even The New York Times recognized that falling incomes rather than tax cuts appear to account for the greatest decline in more taxes paid.

For another example in CT. in 2001, people in the million dollar income bracket or more paid $1 billion in taxes, but paid only $690 million in 2002. (47) That is a $310 million shortfall!! Why? The number of taxpayers with a million dollar income fell from about 7,500 to 5,200. The state and federal government should not rely on volatile stock markets and inconsistent revenue streams. The General Assembly obviously spent this money like a drunken sailor. They started new programs and increased spending on existing programs that become a struggle to maintain when revenues are down. Their only answer is to levy more forms of taxes and raise existing taxes on the millionaires. What a cavalier attitude to have. Because of our mismanagement, we need to tax the people some more.

Under the Clinton administration the federal

government tried this form of taxation with taxing mega yacht owners and jet owners with a $100,000 dollar surtax on each yacht or jet purchased. What happened? The wealthy stopped buying because they wouldn't pay this charge and the industries sunk to such depressed levels, they repealed the tax. Unemployment for yacht and jet manufacturers rose thereby shrinking the tax base and tax revenues were down. When more people are not working, taxes get raised to assist the unemployed. What would happen if millionaires restructured their income to under a million dollars to avoid the tax? This tax would generate less tax revenue for the state.

The liberal legislature is introducing a bill that would increase the tax on millionaires from 1% point, from 5 to 6 percent. Isn't one point from Alcoholics Anonymous that the more you keep doing something and the result is bad, that if one keeps doing it, it does not make it better?!!!

The Governor wants to implement the sin taxes on beer, wine, tobacco etc. What is wrong with this? What would happen if all the smokers and drinkers bought less? Less tax revenue generated for the state. Not only by the purchases of alcohol and tobacco, but by storeowners who pay less in taxes because of declining sales. Just like the luxury tax example on yachts and jets. In a conciliatory sense, the Democrats always like to state these increases will be "temporary," but that is what they said about the income tax. If this proposal passes, and in the future when these tough economic times reoccur, what will there be left to tax? Another scenario is the possibility that the sin taxes will rid the smokers from society. If so, what tax revenue will there be? There will be a tax on not one smoker!

What are needed are sound fiscal policies and tax

revenues that can sustain market fluctuations and down-turns in economic cycles. Implementing tax cuts will enable small businesses to restore some financial loss to levels where re-hiring and then new hiring can happen. With more employees increasing the tax base, tax revenues will increase. Slowing the growth of spending and cutting said expenditures where possible will also help.

Before solutions, allow me to introduce a train of thought from observances on the two party system; and on each of their respective means, or modus operendi for operating and managing the government; be it federal, state or local.

There are two types of people each with their own sets of belief on how to operate the government. On one side you have people who believe it is the power of the people to suggest what is right for themselves and their government. For instance, it is up to the people to tell the government how much tax is too much or just right and to operate the government with what we, the taxpayers give the government. The voters may want a small or large government with certain laws and such. One usually hopes the government respects the wishes of the voters. This is the way it should be. It is up to the government to operate with what the taxpayers give them. The government doesn't tell people how to run their lives, although they want to out of a sense of increasing their empowerment and fostering citizen's dependency on them. Remember, the government employees used to be called "public servants," and these public servants should not receive better wages and benefits than the taxpayers who are paying for their jobs. Much like a chairman approves some but not all of the money a committee requested in its budget with the instruction to make do with what the committee received, the taxpayers should do the same with local, state and the federal government. This is how it should be, the taxpayers work for themselves, not the government. These I would put in the conservative side. If this situation is reversed and taxpayers work for the government, it resembles Mother Russia and socialism too much.

The other side believes it is the government's responsibility to gather up all the illusionary spending projects which create and foster dependency and empowerment and bill the electorate with the cost of running the government by finding every conceivable means to tax the citizens. This "progressive" approach is misleading. Progressive taxes are the lead force behind the redistribution of wealth and thereby steering the country towards socialism. This constitutes the liberal side and the problem with this is the tax on people and corporations become such a burden to cover the initiation and continuity of new spending programs, the economy suffers, consumers have less disposable income to save, invest and spend, government dependency strengthens in numbers and socialism knocks on the door. Vice President Cheney mentioned this scenario in the debate and how Kerry and Edwards belong in this group.

The government wants to re-distribute the wealth through taxation, but this helps create the two tier classes. The government is responsible for this. It is the fiscal and monetary policies over the last hundred years which caused this gap. Free trade policies which have forced rampant unemployment in many industrial and manufacturing sectors have also contributed to this gap. See how these two mechanisms fostered by Globalists have worked together to "Pluck the American Eagle?" The more appropriate means would be to lower everyone's taxes. This would enable more people to keep their hard earned dollars and enhance production. If people work hard and are able to keep more of their money, they would be better off. They would work harder and longer knowing that they would keep the extra money. But, the government doesn't want this. They don't want a return to self reliance and independence. Where would they generate the revenue to spend on programs of their choosing just to empower themselves and to perpetuate their empowerment? Whom would they have to instruct on how to live their lives? These elitist like to sit up there and invoke their ideas on how best the rest of us should live. They will show you how to live and will state they know what is best for you.

As an example of perpetuating their socialistic agenda, I know a Rhodes Scholar indoctrinated with socialistic brainwashing techniques, who when we were discussing taxes, tax rates and progressive taxes, which are just the unquenchable thirst of the government for more money, she remarked progressive taxes are just. Her argument is hey, if Bill Gates makes 30 million dollars a year, he can afford to pay us 70 percent of it. That is the socialist's argument. If you can afford it, it is ours. They grab at an excess. Like the vanity plates in Ct. It used to be a one time fee for the initial cost of making the vanity plates. But, hey, since, the people can afford it once; why not tax them every year!! Sounds great!! More money for us government workers!! It has since been repealed. I just don't understand the mentality that the more you make, the more you get taxed. That does not foster growth and self reliance. So why then are these progressive taxes around? It is a Globalists instrument to gain and maintain control over the masses while empowering their own controlling influences. The government wants everyone to come to them for assistance.

Another example of perpetuation involves one person I know who is Ivy League educated and holds a Master's Degree in International Economics from a venerable graduate school. He once argued that if taxes are too much for the individual worker, then this is good because it forces people to work harder and produce more which would inevitably keep them in their prior standard of living. How bizarre is this argument? He tells me maybe they should work Saturdays to earn the extra money. Well, that is crazy because people are working more now and taking home less. With a progressive tax, if you work more and harder to earn more, more taxes will be taken from your check book. Let's create a scenario, a real one that mocks this train of thought from this International Economist. Two salesmen sit in a bar at happy hour on Friday. They sit around mulling over the idea that tomorrow they have two options; meet here again for more beers and watch whatever sports is on TV, or go to work and try to make a sale, or to be more productive in whatever it is they do. Some people have jobs that prevent working on weekends.

Any salesman can do the math. Let's see, because I get whacked with taxes I don't have as much money, so for me to earn extra dollars to remain in my standard of living, I must work 20 or so weekends, almost 2 a month. If I do make the extra money, I move into a higher tax bracket where the progressive tax takes more of my money and I am left with a few thousand dollars, hardly worth the effort of working 20 weekends, and missing family and leisure time.

This socialistic attitude of high taxes has produced two negative results. It has forced more family members to enter the workforce to sustain their lifestyle. Excessive taxes are also counterproductive.

Don't believe me? As Bruce Bartlett, a Senior Fellow at the National Center for Policy Analysis summarized in his August 11th 2004 article in Investor's Business Daily, the US citizen, while being more productive and taxed less than their European counterparts, makes more money and enjoys a higher standard of living.

According to the Bureau of Labor Statistics, GDP per person in 2003 in 1999 dollars has the US in first place with $34,960. Norway finishes second with $30,882, followed by the UK with $26,039 then France, Italy and lastly Germany with $24,813. From a productive standpoint, the European workers were 86% as productive as the US worker in 1995 and have since dropped to 84% as productive in 2003. This is due mainly because the US worker works more hours. Why? Because they keep most of what they earn as compared to European workers. For instance, Edward Prescott of the Federal Reserve Bank of Minneapolis remarked: "Europe's high taxes explain almost all the difference in labor force participation rates between Europe and the US. When the tax levels are comparable, work hours similar- with higher taxes in Europe, workers respond by working less. Prescott furthers explains that when the tax burden is less, consumption rises. Think back to the earlier example of CT without the income tax, just the sale tax. He further points out that the Europeans feel it doesn't pay to work because welfare benefits are so high, and with the cost of not working so low because after tax money leaves too small a gap to make working worthwhile. So, if lower taxes for US workers work is better than their European counterparts, wouldn't it make sense to cut taxes further to increase production, and consumption?! If lower taxes work better than higher taxes, well, then, let's cut taxes some more!!

When one examines the fallibility of progressive tax rates, is there much difference in a top rate of 39.6% dropping to 36%? On a $100,000 salary, all else being equal, that is only a $3,600 decrease. Will this insignificant tax cut be comparable to Reagan's tax cut and thereby stimulate the economy? Progressive rates reach too high. If one really wants to expand the economy, make the top rate drop to 20%. How and why did Truman's high taxes provide for prosperous times? It was a strong value in the dollar? Taxpayers paid a lot in taxes, but the value of the dollar was strong enough to provide the essentials with mainly one parent working. During Carter's presidency, taxes were almost as high as Truman's, however, because of the declining value in the dollar (first Trade imbalance in 1971), the economy suffered and people struggled to make a living. Because of the dollar's decline, a new trend evolved. For the first time, it became apparent that to buy the necessities and maintain a standard of living, both parents began working. An expensive by product of this is the expense of after school programs, an increase in crime rates because children are home without parental supervision etc.

For an example to show how confiscatory progressive

taxes are, let's review an article in the Hartford Courant by Molly Ivin, "The Trouble With Tax Cuts," Fr. Jan. 10, 2003, she misleads in her math and unfairly denigrates the elderly "Coupon Clippers." Her only accurate statement is that the wealthy do pay the majority of taxes. Tax cuts aren't trouble; outspending revenues is. That is the true reason for CT's financial woes.

While she is correct that the rich get the majority of the tax break, she misleads in asserting it is a break for the rich. Bush's tax break is for everyone, but because the way the math works, she wrongly assumes the non-rich don't get a break as well. For example, in using her numbers, a 10% tax on Person A earning $356,000 and Person B making $73,000 will result in person A paying $28,300 more than person B (35,600-7,300= 28,300.) Since the wealthy are paying more, isn't this amount their "fair share" Molly says they don't pay?

Molly's claim of the "Fair Share" consists of the progressive tax. She believes this scenario is the fairest. It also reveals just how much governments like to steal money from the taxpayers. Molly thinks progressive taxes are fair when under her example person A would pay a 38.6 rate of $137,416 instead of $35,600, or $100,000 more!!. If consumers are not charged for their purchases at progressive rates, how does the federal and state government get away this discrimination? Ct taxpayers already work 136 days a year to pay for taxes. This leaves 120 days left to keep the money for personal expenses. This trend should not be.

If the top 2% pay more than 40% of all federal Income Taxes according to an article by Mr. Jack Kemp citing an IRS statistic, doesn't it make sense that with any tax cut, the higher bracket will receive a larger dollar amount in savings? It is simple math. Legislatures argue that percentage cuts give a larger percentage cut to the low income worker and a small percentage cut to the high brackets in an attempt to even out the dollar amount for all taxpayers. It is trivial and will never work. With an across the board rate reduction the taxes saved by the high-income earner will always be more than the savings of the low-income earner. Therefore, even with the same percentage rate reduction, Person B realizes a smaller dollar amount in tax savings, (Molly's misleading argument) but Person A would still be paying more in taxes, the "fair share."

Using the above example, with an identical across the board tax cut of 2% affecting all brackets, Person A will receive a larger dollar amount in savings yet the rate reduction is the same for all. Person A paying 8% will pay $28,480 in taxes rather than $35,600 for a savings of $7,180 dollars. In comparison, Person B will pay $5,840 in taxes instead of $7,300 for a savings of $1,460 dollars. Person A realized a higher savings because they started with a higher figure. What is important is the rate cut was the same and everyone saved. Don't confuse percentages with dollar amounts; Person A still paid more dollars in taxes.

Secondly, Molly's assertion that only the rich collect dividends and hide them offshore is ridiculous. Government statistics show roughly 50% of the population is invested in the stock market, and if 1% is rich then the other 49% aren't rich but want to become rich, so they would like to receive this dividend tax reduction. Hark back to Lincoln's statement. Why does the current government want to prevent people from making money?

Bush is only trying to increase disposable income for the masses, so the majority of the people can pay bills, save, spend and invest, all good things for reviving the economy. I object to her "coupon clippers" who are either non-working parasites or are trust fund spoiled by grand-daddy's money. How is Molly sure several coupon clippers don't work? Would she rather have these unemployed coupon clippers working and taking a job from someone who really needs the work?

What Molly and many tax hikers believe is similar to the first part of the Chinese proverb while Bush's policy is closer to the second part: "Give a man a fish and you can feed him for a day, teach a man to fish and he can feed himself for life." Taxes too high in which the revenue is spent for subsistence constricts hiring and it would be better for everyone, the company and the individual, to allow the tax cuts to be spent on hiring the person instead. This would foster self reliance, enlarge the tax base and provide for better communities.

The "because you can afford it, we'll tax you" attitude inherent in liberal circles applies to property taxes a well. Take for instances taxes on automobiles. Which group needs, and uses the town's roads the most, the family of 5 with three children in school driving three inexpensive cars or the single millionaire with a Mercedes in the garage? I would say the family needs the roads more. In a comparison, the family which drives three inexpensive cars has 12 wheels versus 4 wheels on the pavement. The millionaire might not be around in the winter, nor would he utilize the school, but his taxes would not reflect that. Because he owns a Mercedes, his taxes on one car will be more than the taxes on the three other cars. Tax officials cannot and should not rely on the assumptive sentiment that the rich will buy the expensive car anyway, or the smokers will pay the tax anyway. After awhile, this sentiment forces rebellion among the victims. What happens to tax revenues when the consumers stop buying the overly taxed items? What happens to tax revenues on expensive cars and cigarettes if people stopped buying them? Wouldn't revenues go down? Wouldn't that hurt the employment of those respective industries? Yes!! Why not implement a fix rate per car? Recall The Whiskey Rebellion, and the luxury tax on yachts and jets.

In a May 2004 Sailing World article, Kimball Livingston pointed out that Maryland's Governor Robert Erlich's proposal of installing a new $50 dollar boat slip tax on boat owners failed only after the boat owners learned the tax revenue would be used to hire government workers. Here is a perfect example of liberal tax-and-spend democrats proposing an unsound economic stimulus to expand government. Suppose this bill had passed, and the Maryland government "created" new jobs by financing them by stealing money in the form of new taxes from taxpayers wealthy enough to own a boat. What would happen if the boat owners sold their boats? Tax revenue decreases, and those "new" jobs become unsustainable. Where would the government find monies to support these jobs if boat owners sold their boats? New taxes? Raise existing ones? What happens is the local, state and federal governments have fewer workers supporting an enlarging government work force? Taxpayers have no money left to be taxed. Governments are not a jobs program!

Same goes for the actual property and the dwelling.

Who should pay more, a big nice house on a half of an acre or a simple modest home on three acres? Which owner has more of the town's land? Shouldn't the three acre homeowner pay more since they own more of the overall land, the proverbial bigger piece of the pie?

What has been recognized among many is that poor people don't want the rich to become poor, they want to get out of poverty and become rich, and it is imperative that the government sets in motion the fiscal policies that would enable that flight from poverty. These fiscal policies are tax breaks, tax incentives so small businesses can hire and remove the citizens dependent on the government into a lifestyle of self sufficiency. High tax rates just keep the poor in poverty. Wages don't make one wealthy, earnings do because one needs to save and invest to remove them from poverty. Wages just help poor people get by.

Using excessive taxes to keep these poor people poor is practically enslaving. It perpetuates the Democratic voting base which is destructive, divisive and all together counter productive to promoting economic growth. It is similar to the Chinese proverb, that after feeding a person for a day, you tax more to feed them for a week rather than propose the Republican philosophy of teaching the person how to fish so they can feed themselves for a life time. The Democrat solution does not make citizens productive, only dependent.

Excessive taxes on Capital Gains, Dividends and Inheritances are another method Globalists use to prevent ordinary citizens from achieving wealth and self sufficiency. Since 50% of the population own stock, wouldn't a tax break or elimination of taxes on dividends seem prudent to increase the disposable incomes of homeowners?

Inheritances taxes are an excellent example of pure government greed. My socialistic Ivy League associate thinks that since the government has provided the means for that person to make all that money, then this inheritance tax is just compensation. How bizarre and what a warped sense of thought! Gee, what were all the progressive taxes they paid during their life considered?! If not totally repealed, then, for any unforeseen catastrophic event where a legal normal transition of ownership could not take place, a balance must be met where an amount of tax could be affordable for families to pay to retain ownership but not too excessive so they lose all.

The benefits of capital gains tax cuts have been shown. They revive the economy because they increase disposable income. As for dividends, among the several methods for corporations to raise capital, two main methods are to borrow from a bank or issue stock. Bank money is paid back in pre tax profits at the rates set by Globalists using their Federal Reserve Bank interest rates. In other words, the interest and principle paid to the bank is tax deductible to the corporation. For an ordinary citizen is this the same on a car loan? No!! One pays for their car loan in after tax dollars! Capital raised by issuing stock is bought by shareholders, or ordinary citizens. In return, corporations pay stockholders dividends for the use of the money, but and this is a BIG but, the dividends are paid in after tax dollars. So it makes sense for corporation to pay the tax deductible bank loan, thereby decreasing their tax liability and leave whatever is left after paying taxes to the stockholders. Does this seem fair? If the Government is so concerned about redistributing the wealth through taxation, why doesn't it redistribute it through dividend tax elimination?!!

In this example, if corporate profits were distributed through dividends, stockholders would make a lot of money, and since 50% of the population is invested, wouldn't this seem to have the biggest impact? Using General Electric as an example, total cash profit per share is over $14.00 dollars yet they pay only an annual .88 cents per share in dividends. Instead of a paltry 88 cents annual dividend a share yielding roughly a 3% return. Why not pay $5 or $10 dollars a share. That would have a huge impact on stockholders and the economy. With dividend payments being pre tax, or tax deductible, corporations should be able to pay more to stockholders. Limit or redistribute executive pay see and infuse this capital as well, and stockholders would be able to achieve some wealth accumulation, enough to remove themselves from some sort of government dependency. With extra dividend income and lower tax rates, disposable income will increase. This is what is needed, because with extra cash, people will save, invest, and spend. These are all good for cash flow, wealth accumulation and reviving an economy. It will also enable the low income taxpayer to break away from government dependency and become more self reliant.

For replacing the income tax, one solution is a progressive flat tax with some provisions seems plausible. First, it would simplify the tax code. Remember, taxpayers are not here to keep an industry of lawyers and accountants employed. The billions of dollars spent on tax preparation could be applied to more productive causes. The tax code is 50,000 pages, larger than the Encyclopedia

Britannica and this is too excessive for any individual to encompass. Taxpayers armed with computers should be able to data entry their taxes bypassing the accountant and send the check in. This is already happening, but too many loopholes create confusion for everyone to do it. While a single Flat Tax rate of 20% would not have a chance to become law, a progressive flat tax would. Progressive rates for incomes could be as follows:

40k and under, 5%.
40k-75k, 7%.
75k-150k, 10%.
150k- 250k, 15%
250k and over, 20%

Unlike standard flat taxes where no deductions are allowed, in this solution, state and property taxes should remain deductible. An amendment establishing a cap where total rates, state and federal combined should not exceed 25% or 30% of income should be in place. Any amount more is confiscatory and slows economy. Married couples with two incomes should not be penalized and should be able to file separately. Married people have more expense and should be given a break. This is easy, simple and eighth grade math. Capital gains and dividend income should be taxed at one rate; preferably 10%, but no higher than 15%. Remember, people invested with after tax dollars with the purpose to accumulate wealth, so let them.

What liberals and progressive tax proponents do not realize is when the higher income bracket gets overtaxed, investment funds for new companies declines as it did when investment dollars collapsed in 2000-2002. Capital

Investment, equipment and software, fell in 8 of the 10 quarters between mid 2000 and end of 2002 with 6 of those quarters being consecutive declines. Investments from this sector transform new ideas into new companies where more people get hired, and more taxes get paid. If Democrats shut off this water hose of dollars, nothing will grow in the garden. Remember what Reagan encountered in the 1980's, when the investment was dismal. He lowered tax rates to increase the investment return on capital and the floodgates of new companies emerged e.g. Microsoft, Oracle, and Home Depot etc.

One other idea is repealing the 16th Amendment and replacing the Income Tax with a "Consumption Tax ". Dismantling the antiquated IRS apparatus will save millions of dollars in the first place and simplify our tax code as well. A proposal on a "Consumption Tax" on the sale of services and foods-for use is an option. With more disposable income, savings and capital formation should increase, stagnation brought on by regressive economic policies will stop, new business will prop up, employment will rise, and more money flowing in the money stream will generate tax revenues through the ability of buying more. On a smaller scale for comparison purposes in the state of CT this "Consumption Tax" is similar to a sales tax, which provided enough revenues in CT to survive for many years. It wasn't until 1992 that Governor Weicker proposed an income tax to fund the states coffers, with the promise to abolish the sales tax, a promise the state did not keep. The revenue/spending situation in CT worsened. The state collects between $300-$400 million dollars a year from a percentage of slot machine revenues from the casinos. Yet CT still has budgetary difficulties.

So, within a span of less than twenty years, the economic climate has fallen to where the state imposed an income tax, a means to collect casino revenues, a conveyance tax, kept intact the sales tax, enlarged the gas tax and somehow barely manages to keep afloat? How did CT survive with just a sales tax? Tax and trade policy eroded the tax base and increased government dependency. How does this state represent a larger national problem?

States can adopt a similar consumption tax and collect the revenue and forward it on the national government on a quarterly basis. This will create more individual economic freedom, which is exactly what the Globalists don't want. They want to dominate people in such a way as to force these people into submission. Are individuals working for themselves, or are they working for the government and hence the Globalists.

The Globalists like to create a waste program to tax us more to support these waste programs. Take for instance war, drug wars, welfare, environmentalism, a war on health care, a war on education and war on poverty in which we have spent $5 trillion dollars since the war began over 30 years ago during Johnson's "Great Society." To pay for all these wars, they tax us on our incomes, which are our rewards for our hard work and productive spirit. A tax on consumption would remove the tax on production, it will tax on spending derived from hard work, inheritance etc. This will reduce the taxes on those working to earn incomes through productive labor. If a person does not consume much, or is not frivolous with purchase decisions, they will realize an increase in savings. It all comes full circle. Now, people have already figured out not to work any harder if taxes will increase for said labor.

I have spoken of the "Lag time" when discussing the Interest Rates and their impact on society. Any decrease in Interest Rates will not have an immediate impact on employment, much to the delight of liberals and to the uninformed citizen who disbelieve this mechanism just as they dislike like a tax cut to revive the economy, When decreases occur, at least 6 to 12 months and up to 18 months are required for them to make their impact known. It is during this time the Liberals berate the Republicans that the Interest Rate cuts and tax cuts are not helping.

What is happening is business needs to forecast future growth and they estimate over a quarter, (3 months to a quarter) and a quarter to business is nothing when compared to an unemployed citizen? When rates drop, companies will run financial analysis to learn of loan affordability. They use future sales forecasts and results take time. Wait for next quarter's results they shout. By the time the company receives the loan for plant expansion or technological improvement, and generates sales and receives sales revenues, a year can go by before the company hires new employees.

What is needed is a fiscally sound tax policy that can weather the volatile revenues from Wall Street and economic cycles that is simultaneously fair and equitable for everyone without hindering economic stimulation and enlarging government dependency. Promoting means to increase disposable income for all taxpayers is essential. Government can achieve this by legislating tax cuts on all incomes and by simplifying the tax code. For individual tax rates, across the board tax cuts work. Overall, this supply side practice which worked before provides more disposable income that increases a family's ability to save, invest, and buy. In a Republican held Congress Clinton did sign into law a 25% Capital Gains Tax break. Wasn't this part of the "Gingrich Revolution?" Did not prosperity follow in the late 1990's? Wasn't this the same remedy as applied by Reagan and Kennedy? Of course it was!

As mentioned in a Lawrence Kudlow article and supported in the recent 2004 presidential debates, the wealthiest individuals who make over $200,000 dollars a year comprise roughly 70% of all small businesses. Since the small businessman is the engine that revives the economy by hiring many new employees, isn't it prudent to give them a break to jumpstart their recovery? Yet, Bill Clinton remarked at the Democratic Convention that these wealthy people don't need this money, as if it is all right to tax (steal) more of their money. How preposterous!!

The same is true with taxes. When Bush signed his tax cuts, there were no immediate results either; again, much to the delight of the liberals. They screamed and shouted all through the campaign that the tax cuts are not working. Even though the tax cuts may be realized in the paycheck, the typical citizen will wait to after April 15 to learn how much money they have gained. It is only after tax time and the time to clean up their household finances do citizens spend and save their money. Again, like the Interest Rate, the lag time for tax cuts take some time, in this case almost a year. What are the results?

In an October 19 article in the Investor's business Dailey, statistics show the tax cuts are having the positive and desired effects. First, a lag time for taxes to cause a positive effect on the economy takes time. Companies, like people, need some tax breaks to clean up their personal finances before they can expand and invest. Bush wants this. The results of his tax cuts are better than expected.

The $1.8 trillion tax cut has pulled the economy out of the recession. The US has added more than $1 trillion to the Gross Domestic Product. The most recent quarter shows GDP grew at a 3.7% pace and since the tax cuts have taken root, GDP has grown at a 4.6% rate. Both figures compare quite nicely with the 3.2% average since 1970. Inflation is down to the lowest levels in 40 years; unemployment is down to 5.4%, just a little better than the 5.8% average of the 1990's and much better than the over 6% rate of the 70's and 80's. Corporate profits, factory orders, household wealth and median home prices are all up, indicating the second Bush term is poised for economic prosperity. I am just glad Bush won other wise Kerry would have set in place measures to reverse these promising numbers.

One Nobel Prize winner remarks that Bush did not cut taxes enough.

History has proven supply side economics' practice of tax cuts generate economic expansion by increasing disposable income as they did in the 1920's, 1960's, and 1980's Excessive taxes play into the hands of the Globalists who spread socialism across the globe while the US taxpayer pays for it. If you support the Globalists' plan, then be prepared for excessive taxes and socialism. If you want to have a better life at home, demand tax cuts and keep the money here in the US.

How much has the political spectrum shifted to the left? During his July speech in Berlin, Barack Obama mentioned that we are citizens of the world and must eradicate global poverty. If elected, a bill he sponsored,

The Global Poverty Act, steers the US down a global socialist destiny. He believes it is a priority of American foreign policy to eliminate global poverty, provide shelter and drinking water to every child.

Paying for these lofty goals is another matter. Obama cites his legislation which refers to the "millennium development goal" a declaration for the United Nations Millennium Assembly of 2000. In this declaration, paying for this "war on poverty" would be paid by the redistribution of the wealth of land, and of the world's resources. This amounts to an additional 0.7% of gross domestic product on top of the $16.3 billion dollars the US already spends on fighting poverty. Instead of introducing capitalism and democracy where people learn skills and develop a middle class, this amounts to hand outs; similar to the adage of giving a person a fish instead of teaching them how to fish. This would create even larger government dependency.

Obama went further stating that we, the US citizens, can't keep driving SUV's and heating our homes at 72 degrees and force the rest of the world to accept it. Here is another example of the government trying to tell the citizenry how to live, the lowering of our side of the seesaw example to a level playing field with the lesser developed countries. Will or should we, as US citizens allow China or India to tell us not to load up the SUV and look for a cheeseburger while driving to the beach? I can hear the orders from the government, I am sorry Mr. and Mrs. Jones, I know you have planned this summer beach vacation for a year, but driving a few hundred miles in your SUV is not allowed anymore. How will this go over with the tax paying citizens?

How has over taxation affected the US population? In a contrasting viewpoint about taxes, researchers at the Economic Mobility Project concluded that in today's world the relationship of adult sons income, when compared to their parents, the US lags behind France, Germany, Canada, Sweden, Finland, Norway and Denmark in a measure of upward mobility. Most recently, several European countries have cut taxes, which have created more disposable income, which in turn has kept the US economy afloat by buying our exports!! This scenario is occurring when some of these countries are socialistic anyway, with over 50% to 70% taxation and with more time off from work...think of Europeans taking the month of August off. Yet, these countries' young adults are seeing a brighter future than their respective parents than young adults in the US. Why is this happening?

Studies went further revealing that young workers in their 30's in 2004 earned 12% less than the 30 year old workers in 1974. In 1974, the US was in the midst of an energy crisis,, malaise of the 70's and despite this, still earned more than today's young adults!! How? Spreading dollars cause inflation which eventually devalues the dollar. The research found the American family stays afloat because of the women's paycheck.

So, during the pre 1970's, pre trade deficit, pre removing the dollar from the gold, the household with dad working, as portrayed in the 1970 sitcoms about life in the 1950's, Leave it to Beaver, and Happy Days as examples provided enough for the family. In thirty short years, the situation has deteriorated to having both parents work and barely getting by.

Need more evidence? In an Investor Business Daily's

article on Dec. 9, 2008, IRS data pointed out that in 1980, the top 1% earned 8.5% of all adjusted gross income but paid 19% of all the taxes. However, by 2006, that same group made 22% of AGI but paid 40% of overall taxes. Conclusion is their tax rates rose faster than their income grew.

In a Nov. 10, 2008 piece, the IBD provided a chart showing four columns; the income tax receipts, total tax receipts, federal outlays and non defense spending, as percentages of Gross Domestic Product.. From 1941, the income tax receipts range from 5% to 8%, total tax receipts remain consistent as well ranging from 14%-18%. With the exception of WWII, the total federal outlays remained in the high teens. The big difference resides in the non-defense spending category, where during WWII, it totaled 6% but in the next 60 years until 2007 has climbed to 16% of GNP. Where is the government spending this additional money? They are spending our tax dollars on welfare provisions, and illegal immigrant programs!! The US is becoming a nanny state. We are spending a higher percentage on non-defense spending programs because illogical trade and monetary policy created ramifications which lead to increased taxes to provide for the government dependents!

Still not convinced, or at least a little bit suspicious. Years later, after the McCarthy hearings in July 1953, the committee appointed Norman Dodd to investigate the Tax –Exempt Foundations. During the investigation, Dodd was asked by the President of the Ford Foundation, Rowan Gather, to visit. According to Dodd, Gather remarked, the substance of these directives for the foundation, is as follows: "We shall use our grant-making power to alter life in the United States so that it can be comfortably merged with the Soviet Union." (48) One foundation that came under investigation by Dodd was the Carnegie Foundation. In 1908, (Before taxation, doesn't it seem strange or did the Globalists know taxation was coming and put in place and protected their groups beforehand?!) Dodd was allowed to read and examine the minutes of the Trustee meetings and discovered that the board concentrated on an academic discussion on whether there was any means more effective than war to alter the life of the people of a nation. Examples of fostering war have appeared in other sections. Think of the Spanish American War and the "need" for taxes to pay for it. Think of the attempts of world government, League of Nations and the United Nations post world wars respectively. The Tax-Exempt Foundations illustrate the Socialist goals of the Globalists. These Foundations support the political and economic policy makers in Washington with editorials and interviews. It is easy for a voter to call a political or economic advisor's solution unwise, but if a Foundation supports the argument, how can the public disagree. Or, the politicians can accept and recommend socialistic agendas from these foundations. Either way, socialistic agendas get pushed down citizen's throats.

Health Care

On a cold and snowy evening in late December in 1931, a young Doctor ventured out in a blizzard to make a house call. During his ten minute walk, he reflected on his new career. Having just finished his residency, he looked forward to beginning his new career with this patient because this patient was his first. It was his first patient because he was the only one available on New Years Eve. It helped that he did know the patient, but nonetheless, they called and he responded. After delivering the baby, the doctor trekked back home with $50 in cash in his pocket, his fee for delivering the baby. Thus, he started a trend of working during any holiday, evening or weekend, for he realized the obvious: the more people he saw, the more money he could earn. In a short time, as the doctor's practice grew, he realized several people paid by the other means, meat, fruit, clothes, usually in the commodity of what ever business the family worked. In any event, the doctor realized in a short time that he received full payment immediately upon services rendered or shortly thereafter.

Fast forward almost 70 years to 1998. On a hot summer evening, an elderly doctor was awoken by that all too often sound of an endlessly ringing phone. By one AM, he was driving the forty minutes to the hospital to perform an emergency operation. By all accounts, he reflected positively that that was all. There was no trauma to speak of, nor car accidents nor gunshot wounds that kept him in the hospital all evening. Those types of patients were

usually the ones that don't care too much about themselves anyway. Taking care of people in drunken brawls,
gunfights, knife fights and drug inflicted accidents got frustrating. It tested the Doctors Hippocratic Oath of taking
care of all people regardless of race, religion and payment
etc. He had no problem with providing the treatment, it
was that he usually saw these same people on another evening in the Emergency Room with another wound and
since they had no health insurance, the care was a freebee
courtesy of the hospital and him. This was also not one of
his nor his partner's patients in the emergency room suffering some form of post operative discomfort. This was
a simple and routine appendectomy, although being an
emergency, he still took it seriously. The doctor surmised
if all goes well, he should have no problem and should be
home in a few hours. He was just covering the Emergency
Room for the evening. These "on call" situations get very
tedious to doctors so, while he was glad no one was truly
serious, he was tired of these trips especially when retirement was six months away.

Upon arrival, the patient was being prepared for surgery, for emergency appendectomies do not wait. However, the doctor was delayed because the patient's healthcare provider needed to be informed of the operation, to
approve of the operation and give consent to the doctor
performing the operation. In other words, some hospital
employee had to call an HMO employee, usually some
young non medically trained person in front of a computer clicking and double clicking throughout their data
base to make sure everything was ok and in order before
the Doctor could operate. In the meantime, during the
waiting period for approval, the patient's appendices can

rupture, risking death, and the Doctor would have to violate procedure and operate anyway. He can get sued for doing this. He can also get sued if he followed procedure, waited for approval and the patient died. Anxiety like this forces doctors to retire early.

Anyway, the Doctor receives approval, he operates, and the patient survives. All goes well, except, this half hour procedure took the better part of the evening, and he returns home in time for breakfast. Unlike the doctor in the previous example this one didn't get paid. He won't get paid until six months down the road; after he retires. He didn't even get fruit or meat, or some equitable trade of goods or services from the patient. A short time later, he is notified by the HMO that he will receive payment, but not the full payment he billed. He later received $132.00 for a $600.00 bill. Even the $600 dollar bill is inadequate. For example the doctor in this example charged $250 dollars for the same operation upon returning from Vietnam in 1967 and charged and received in full $400 dollars shortly thereafter. According to the Consumer Price Index, the dollar value in today's money of a $400.00 1967 bill correlates to a bill for an approximate amount of $2,000.00; far below his standard thirty years ago. Imagine some other profession that would work for fees that existed 30 years ago! Would a lawyer? No! Would an accountant prepare your taxes for rates of 30 years ago? No! Mechanic, Barber? All no. You get the picture.

He laments and relates to me the story, laughs, and states he can't wait to retire. He shakes his head because not only did he not receive full payment, the HMO payment does not even cover his expenses. He figures he lost out of pocket over $300 dollars. He recounts how he arrived at this loss. He figures for each operation per year, he needs $400 to cover expenses; $200 for malpractice insurance, and $200 for office expenses to break even. Any amount over the $400 for an operation is for him, so he lost money on the emergency appendectomy. The doctor had to spend his out of pocket money to the tune of $72 to cover mal practice and $200 to pay for his expenses. So, instead of receiving $600 which would have netted him $200, this doctor paid $272 for the luxury of operating on this patient for free in the middle of the night. Yet, with all of these headaches, it is no wonder that doctors are leaving their profession.

Somehow, he has to find money to pay his nurses, pay his rent and pay his malpractice, without which he could not work in the first place. One doctor related to me that after he calculated the math for a years worth of work, he kept the money he made for two months work. That means the money he earned from the other ten months worth of work was applied to expenses. He can't pass on expenses to the patient like other businesses do to consumers and clients. If this patient suffers some sort of post operative-discomfort, will he sue the doctor? Do people sue a mechanic, a lawyer, for not doing a good job or for losing a case? In today's world, how does a doctor maintain his sanity, not worry about expenses, withstand the fear of lawsuits and somehow keep a clear head so they can provide astute care in treating patients. With all of these negative issues, it is no wonder to see what is wrong with health care in this country. Notice I did not say medical care. Medical care is great in this country when compared to other countries. It is the health care aspect, the administering of the medical care that is driving up costs, forcing doctors to leave the profession and causing undo strain on patients, taxpayers and strangles business.

Webster's definition of Socialized Medicine is "medical and hospital services for the members of a class or population administered by an organized group (as a state agency) and paid for from funds obtained by assessments, philanthropy or taxation." The US Government calls it "Universal Health Care." We should call it what it really is, "Socialized Medicine"!!

So what has happened to the medical profession in the last century that has the doctor in example one being respected and paid on time for services, to the doctor in example two who has become a body mechanic? How did we end up where we are?

How do we reverse the trend of ever increasing health care cost which are on the brink of coming under federal control and socialized medicine? What happened to Doctors and what happened to health care that has made it so expensive in this country? How did we get to where we are today and what can be done to resolve this "health care crisis?" How do we make life or should I say, the caring for life simpler, easier on the patients, nurses, and doctors. How do we prevent the government from socializing this aspect of our lives? How do we limit or abolish the health care bureaucracy so it doesn't turn into another cabinet position, thereby removing all health care decisions from where it matters most; from the people involved, the patients and their doctors to a government bureaucracy? How do we prevent the government from making health decisions for the people; a choice of care where it used to belong, with the people?

How Medicine Used to Work to Present Day.

Prior to World War II, medicine and health care were a practice, and the doctor sent a bill and the patient paid either through their insurance company or by themselves. It worked fine. Any patient that could not afford full payment, installment plans were arranged or some barter system was negotiated, but the doctor received "full payment." For instance, if the patient owned a butcher shop, half of the bill might be paid in cash and the other half might be free meat for two months. This worked brilliantly. Both people in the transaction, the patient and the doctor, were satisfied. Neither third parties, nor any forms to fill out were involved; everyone was happy. In several cases, doctors used their discretion and didn't send a bill, their prerogative. With all the forms in today's medical profession, doctors find it hard to offer this gesture.

In any case, the doctor received his full pay in cash or a financial equivalent in some goods or services. If the insurance company paid only a portion of the bill, the patient paid the balance. In complete destitute cases, the doctor did what they all have sworn to do and forgave payment. That was okay to do because the doctor could afford to provide the free care to those in need because since his fee was economically appropriate for the time and he received full payment from all the other patients, his accounts receivable reached a level where he could provide care for the less fortunate at no costs. Call it medical pro bono work. In today's world Lawyers can provide pro bono work because of their fees, not so with Doctors.

In the first example, the family with a pregnant woman saved money to pay the doctor. How many people save today for the impending birth of a child? Parents save money to re-style the bedroom; they save and buy the needed baby equipment, strollers, cribs etc, but does anyone ever save to pay a doctor? People save to buy a car. People save to buy a home. People save to buy expensive items, but does anyone really stop to save to pay a doctor. No. They expect medical care for free. Let someone else pay for it, I want to buy something nice, say a vacation or flat screen TV the sentiment goes. Maybe it is because hospitals are not a business and people need to spend money on consumer goods to turn the economic cycle to generate sales and profits and fulfill Wall Street expectations. I am not sure, but everyone expects health care to be free. Well, as a friend of a doctor, I want my legal fees and accountant's fees to be free! See how well that goes over if ever proposed to Congress.

In many cases, the patient was so thankful, they presented the doctor with certain gifts above and beyond the full payment as a thanks, or a tip much the way cops get a free cup of coffee at a diner, a barber receives a tip for taking a good customer on short notice or without an appointment or a mechanic shop gets some coffee and doughnuts from a customer to ensure quality and timely repair on their car. The doctors were the good guys like the doctors you see in movie westerns, respected and given preferential treatment in return for the doctor's efforts. That all changed after World War II. With the advent of Blue Cross becoming the main responsibility for all medical payments, the Doctor's lives and health care slowly began to change for the worse.

As for the hospitals, patients usually enjoyed longer Hospitals visits; the expense was negligible when compared to today's costs. Why? Currently, the hospitals rush a patient in the day of an operation and get you out as fast as possible, regardless if health requires a longer stay. Hospitals need to watch the bottom line and there is only so much money for insurance companies to spread to every conceivable patient. How did we come from a time when a mother could give birth and remain in the hospital for a week or more to today's world where she leaves the same day? Medical technology? Perhaps. Bottom line, of course. What happens if the patient wants to stay an extra night, will pay for it and is refused? Is this scenario the correct way of treating patients? What happened?

As the post war economy started to boom in the fifties, the citizens wanted to take advantage of all the good things in life; cars, homes vacations etc. That was fine but people still got hurt, sick, pregnant or whatever and needed a doctor and a hospital. When a corporation bought Life Insurance, D & O, Liability, Workers Compensation etc, as long as the corporation purchased from one provider, the provider included health for little or no extra cost. The insurance company, by law, had to offer health insurance, not because health might have been used as an incentive to buy from one provider, but the law stipulated that an insurance company had to offer all forms of insurance. They could not sell some forms of insurance such life and home and omit health. Insurance companies were a one stop shop for all of the consumer's needs. With the insurer collecting premiums on Life, D & O, Fire, etc. the insurer could "Throw In" Health Insurance at minimum costs. As "Baby Boomers" needed health care, these outlays became higher than the Insurance Companies expected. In an attempt to keep a healthy bottom line, insurance companies could not afford to cover the "full payment" for doctors. They mailed a percentage of the total bill to the patient where the doctor hoped would be forwarded on; and the remaining balance would have to be made up by the patient. However, people did one of two things. They either mailed the percentage check from Blue Cross directly to the doctor without the balance being paid or they just pocketed the check and never paid the doctor. Whatever they did, the doctor got ripped off. Try doing this to an auto mechanic. Tell him the bill is too high, have an outside payment company pays you directly, not the dealership, intending it to be applied to the mechanic's bill, and drive your car out of the lot. Sure, that'll happen!

To correct this problem, the Doctors asked Blue Cross if the checks could be mailed directly to them instead of to the patient thinking 80% of something is better than 100% of nothing. In order to make this deal work, Blue Cross coerced the Doctors to accept the check only if it were for "full payment." This minor concession was actually a major turning point in the medical profession and had an everlasting and devastating effect on Doctors. This act transferred the responsibility of payment from the patient to the insurance companies. The patient no longer had a bill to pay, nor a balance of a bill. They were removed from the equation. The doctor billed directly to the insurance company. Throughout the 1950's and 1960's, this appeared to work adequately, meaning, as Doctor's fees and the medical expenses rose due to normal economic cycles, the insurance companies were able to meet the financial costs of both parties.

Medicaid and Medicare was the product of President Johnson's Great Society suggesting that universal lifelong health care is a birthright. If this does not seem unreasonable, then let Congress pass a law granting similar "Birthright" provisions in legal, and accounting fields. Let congress devise the means to arrange for an HMO like middleman for lawyers. Imagine how all the lawyers would feel if all of their work were pro bono, fees regulated by an outside party and restrictions on how to practice. One can draw similarities in all professional and service fields, from accountants, to auto dealers, to painters, plumbers and electricians. No one individual in any of the above groups would approve, like or adhere to it. People strike for less then these infringements on doctors.

As costs for both hospital care and Doctor's fees increased in the latter part of the 1970's, insurance companies began to feel the financial strain of making payments. Something had to be done. One faulty corrective measure was to cut the doctor's payment from 100% to 80%. As you previously read, the percentage of receipts to the actual bill has dropped dramatically. Doctors now receive less than 50% of what they charge and should be able to bill according to the consumer price index.

When Health Care expenses rose to unmanageable levels, thanks to the added burden brought on by the Great Society, the Government devised the expensive and corrective measure to begin the bureaucracy that the government wanted in the first place, Socialized Medicine, and so it developed and promoted the Health Maintenance Organization, or HMO's.

Realizing the unpopularity of introducing "Socialized Medicine," the Globalists used a less threatening name called the new health care bureaucracy the Health Maintenance Organizations. Here is another example of the small steps taken by the Globalists; they know they cannot flip a switch to Socialism, but need to steer the population like a ship towards its final destination, unbeknownst to the passengers. That's is what HMO's have done.

So, while the initial intentions seemed plausible, future expenses and ramifications were not examined, and the "Chaos" scenario arose which forced the socialistic safety net of Government supervision.

Health Maintenance Organizations

How did the government sell the concept of HMO's to the public? Easy, they created a crisis situation, the aforementioned "Chaos" that allows it to gain control of an industry, in this case the medical industry through government assistance in helping insurance companies pay. In this case Insurance Companies would let it be known that rising medical costs are costing too much and we need some assistance. They create situations on each sector of health care: the patients, the doctors, and the hospitals that adversely affect their respective attitude toward medical care, create a stir in public opinion so everyone throws up their arms in disgust, and screams "Why can't the government just take care of it." When this "Collective Cry" erupted in late 1970's, early 1980's the government's first step in the mission to socialize medicine was accomplished. Since the Government could not force socialistic concepts upon the citizens, knowing it would be unacceptable, they created a "chaos" scenario where the citizens actually begged the government to take care of the problem they created themselves. The government led the people to their own demise. They stole Health Care from the private sector and incorporated it into their own bureaucracy!!

Insurance paid in full a doctor's bill. Up until the late 1970's pre HMO, insurance companies provided all types of insurance; it was the law. If an insurance company sold auto, life, home, fire, they also had to offer health. They could not be in business by selling some policies and not all. So, when companies bought insurance and benefits for their business, employee's health insurance was "thrown in" in this blanket coverage. The premiums for all other forms of insurance covered the health care expenses for employees. The insurance companies could afford the full payment of the real fee and pay it in a timely fashion, usually within 10 business days.

As the health care liabilities continued to rise, the insurance companies used their considerable lobbying efforts and changed the law and divested themselves from "Having" to sell health insurance. Insurance Companies could still sell Life, Home and Auto, but Health was dropped. A void appeared in who was to provide health insurance and the Government proposed Health Mainte-nance Organizations, a precursor to socialized medicine. So the Insurance Companies divested themselves from the high expenses in their budgets, the medical portion, and pawned it off on the government.

HMO's were supposed to be the saviors of the med-ical profession. These managerial stars from business schools and other existing businesses were going to show everyone, especially doctors how to manage the health care industry. Besides, doctors are "dumb" businessmen right! Wrong, doctors know how to run their industry but they don't have the time. The HMO's were going to save money, restrain the upward spiraling costs of health care through their cost cutting business practices, they were going to provide affordable health care for all and make everyone happy! Right? Wrong! All HMO's have done is make a bad situation worse. They are one of the main contributors to rising health care costs while simultaneously increasing the dissatisfaction among health care professional and patients.

The doctors would like to set their own rates and receive full payment for those rates just like any other profession, but they don't. For example, a doctor would bill for an operation, fair and just based on current rates of $1,600.00. Medicare will mail a letter to the patient writing the "usual and customary" rate may be $900.00. Medicare has performed two injustices here. One, they are cheating the doctor out of $700.00 and secondly, they are misleading the patient into believing the doctor is overcharging them $700.00. Medicare arrives at this rate in a budgetary and actuarial method; they divide the number of these types of operations by the budget for these types of operations, regardless of what the doctor wants to charge. Medicare then has the patient pay the $100.00 deductible and then pays 80% of the remaining $800.00 or $640.00. This $740.00 total is drastically less than the $1,600.00 originally billed, and less than the previously mentioned 50 percent. Try applying these calculations to other professions; it would not be accepted. Ask lawyers why they take 33% when real estate agents only take 6%? If people are entitled to free health care, should people be entitled to free legal care?!

How did HMO's adversely affect patients? HMO adversely affect the public financially, and affects the decision making process which negatively affects the care. As the situation is today, citizens and businesses contribute premiums to a HMO for medical care. The HMO's collect huge sums of money out of which they use to pay hospitals and doctors. Where Blue Cross has a 5-8% overhead, HMO's have a 40-50% overhead, so for every dollar paid into the program, almost half gets applied to health care. The other half covers the payroll for the HMO's; the people employed but who have no knowledge of and don't administer health care to the patient. This is roughly 50 cents of every $1 dollar of health care premium wasted already. As costs increase, HMO's do two things; they cut doctor's fees and pass the expenses onto businesses and people or both.

We have already seen how a doctor's fees have shrunk. The $132 dollars a doctor made should have been conservatively $2,000 when inflation is added and according to similar prices then and adjusted to present day values. Secondly, do HMO's think of layoffs in their own industry? Doubtful! Do they cut their million dollar salaries? No way! When health care costs too much, companies don't hire, unemployment rises, self employed people drop coverage, all leading to the increase of the uninsured in this country. This phenomenon increases the dependency on HMO's and the government. The Washington bureaucrats want this, the more and more dependency, the bigger the bureaucracy becomes. When it gets too big, it is too big to abolish, and when this happens, the government can steer the industry towards socialization.

In an April 14th piece, a doctor reveals the gluttoness monetary appetite of healthcare providers, notably, Anthem Health Insurance. In his article, Dr. Joyce writes that the cost of health insurance he provides to his employees is increasing 18.2%. He further notes that the compensation package of Anthem's Chief Executive, a Mr. Larry Glassock will be $42.5 million dollars. This doctor, like all doctors are watching their payments from HMO's decrease, while health care executive's salaries increase and all at the expense of the patients. He finishes with how this $42.5 million package could be spent on patients: nearly a million office visits, 77,000 carpel tunnel surgeries, 20,000 hip replacements or 71,000 MRI's. Is the HMO's Chief Executive going to perform some sort of health care service for his $42 million dollars? NO! Does he operate? No! Does he draw blood? No, so why should he be paid for health care when he doesn't provide it?

Reviewing the finances of HMO's, one discovers vast waste or misallocation of resources. Writing from my home state of CT, I know of six HMO's that are headquartered here. In March of 2003, the Hartford Courant reported that the HMO's earned $102 million dollars in 2002. As of Oct. 31 of this year, Aetna's Health Care reported $179 million dollars of operating earnings. How much of the premiums are spent on HMO's salaries, wages, expenses and not on the medical care of the person responsible for the premium. Doesn't this seem like a waste? Michael Bell, the CFO of Cigna expects the medical costs to rise 11-12% next year while simultaneously stating he forecasts a 10-11% shrinking enrollment in the health plan. So now the situation can only get worse; cover the ever increasing medical costs of those former enrolled by passing the burden of the increase onto a shrinking number of payees of premiums. Not one person in the HMO put a band-aid on a patient in a hospital. I bet a lot of you are happy to learn where all those premium dollars are going. That is $42 million profit, plus payroll, plus salaries, plus expenses, total over hundreds of millions of dollars just in CT that are NOT being applied to health care.

In a recent Hartford Courant article, it was predicted that health care costs will rise 6.7% next year and that insurance companies plan on shifting this expense onto the workers in two ways. First, they want to increase the contribution to the plan from workers and secondly to increase the deductibles. Both ideas are bad. They are asking employees to increase premium payments, i.e. contribute more from their paycheck so less take home and disposable income, on one hand and increase the deductible on the other, so by the time employee needs insurance, more of his health care will be paid for by the employee anyway. Added to this is the 26% Medicare cut in payment to doctors which makes this arrangement more profitable for HMO's and Insurance Companies. What the HMO's and Insurance companies have done is expand on both sides the payment spectrum of the employees which diminishes their liability thereby decreasing the amount of money they pay. By reducing their liability, the HMO's are able to keep more of the premium dollars.

This same article states in CT, the average cost of providing health insurance is over $9,300 and nationally, this figure is over $7,500 per person for eye, dental and medical. I personally can get my eyes checked and teeth cleaned for under $500 per year. I am contributing more of my money, and my company's money to pay the salaries of HMO's!! Premium payments do not match the quality of care. Where does the money go? If I weren't taxed as much, and if restructuring of health care premiums were devised, and if monies spent on premiums went directly to doctors, and hospitals, then the doctors would be able to care for the less fortunate, and citizens like myself would not mind. People are used to paying a "Service call" for a contractor just to show up at your house before any work gets done; why can't this principle be applied to medicine?

The next negative impact on patients affects the doctors as well. Patients routinely complain that their doctors don't spend enough time with them. They complain the doctor saw me for five minutes and ran off and charged me $100 for the visit. The situation has become an economy of scale example. Well, the doctor may have charged the patient, but the patient won't be paying, the HMO will and payment will probably be half of what the doctor charged. From the doctor's viewpoint, they will receive only a portion of the $100 dollars so they don't have the time they want to spend with each patient. When HMO's decrease doctor's pay, doctors lose money, and they need to make up the difference in volume of patients examined. Instead of visiting and spending quality time with 10 patients paying $100 each, doctors have to rush from appointment to appointment to see twice as many patients who are now receiving HMO payment for half. Essentially, HMO's threw out the doctor's bedside manner. Not what the patient wants nor is it the way doctor's want to practice medicine. Doctors nowadays cannot afford the bedside manner. Here you have the bureaucratic HMO's getting what they want; the patient and doctors fighting about time spent for the appointment and the dollar amount charged. Eventually blame gets passed on to the HMO's which gives them the excuse to become a bigger bureaucracy by convincing Congress to throw more money at the problem. It is a program of self perpetuating empowerment.

Lastly, for the patients, filling out paper work and finding your doctor in the right HMO plan that works at a hospital near you is too cumbersome an ordeal. Everyone has been through this nightmare process. Trying to match the HMO most suitable for you, with your preferred doctor and hospital of choice is burdensome and frustrating. The HMO's force you to decide what is best for them, not for the consumer or doctor. Eventually, this limitation in decision making forced HMO to be accommodating to patient's wishes, but adversely affected the doctors. For doctors to retain patients and therefore ensure getting paid, they needed to enroll in all or all most all of the HMO's. This blanket coverage for doctors is insane. One corporation enrolled in 14 HMO's, just so the majority of their patients can remain seeing their doctors. Doctor's then have to hire another non medical person, ever increasing office overhead, just to manage the paper work of billing and accounts receivable from 14 different HMO's

One strong method HMO's use to destroy the doctor's will to continue practicing medicine is their involvement, hence delay, in just that, the practicing of medicine. Doctor's should not have to call the HMO's for permission to operate. This often causes too many delays. How rational is it anyway when a doctor phones this person who sits in front of a computer miles away and who doesn't even examine the patient first hand then punches into the computer the diagnosis and relays these answers and confirmations back to the doctor. How well this works is an example here.

This one doctor was to operate on an elderly lady on a Wednesday. On Tuesday, she arrived at the hospital for blood tests. Knowing that some people, especially the elderly get lightheaded after giving blood, the doctor casually suggested and she accepted the offer to remain in the hospital for the evening. For heavens sakes, he would be operating on her the next day. No problem? Wrong!! Problem. The HMO disallowed her staying at the hospital and ordered her to go home. Well, while home, she fell, hit her head and broke her hip. She was rushed to the hospital where this same doctor and an orthopedic surgeon took care of her. Now she was in the hospital for a few weeks, costing a lot more money than her original desire of an overnight stay would have cost. The doctor finally performed the original operation six weeks later. Her initial condition was complicated and delayed treatment for her fainting accident, she endured more pain caused from the delay and cost her and the HMO thousands of dollars more than originally planned had she stayed overnight. Sounds like HMO's know how to treat a patient.

To put it into perspective, this would be akin to having a group of people unknowledgeable about cars controlling the auto mechanics and dealers in the country. People would contribute money to the group, and this group would decide when to get your car fixed, where it was going to be fixed, fixed by whom and decide how much the dealer and the mechanic would get paid. Yeah, that would go over real well. Imagine the reaction of the car industry if this group could justifiably state to the dealers that they make too much money for selling this car and we will decrease your profits and by the way the hourly charge for your mechanics is too high, you'll only get paid this much. By enforcing HMO policy, the people's choice of hospital, doctor and care is decided by the HMO and not by the people involved, where it belongs, with the patient and their doctor.

Imagine what would happen in professional sports if the athletes were treated like doctors? Fans travel to the ball park to see the players much like a patient travels to the hospital to visit a doctor. Now imagine an organization like the umpires that instructs the owners how to operate their stadiums and teams; an organization that legislates ballplayers' salaries. When confronted with salary issues, the players strike. What would happen in the health care arena if doctors went on strike like ballplayers do for the reason of inadequate compensation?!!! Who would provide the health care? The hospital with too many over paid executives? The HMO employees and executives? Fans go to ball parks to watch the players, not the owners and not the umpires. If fans are willing to pay higher ticket prices to watch their favorite players, why can't patients pay for or payment be made to the doctors. Fans pay the higher prices but the monies do get distributed in salaries to the players, but this is unlike the medical profession where the salaries for the HMO and hospital executive rise at the expense of doctor's salaries shrinking.

Imagine doctors striking like professional athletes who do strike because of inadequate compensation. Operations will not begin, people will die. Bone fractures will not be set and healed, and people will live with deformity.

Forcing the doctors to accept the full payment scheme from Blue Cross back in the 1950's, was the beginning of the end for doctors. This first step now is built in to the mind set of the public and doctors. Now that the government has control over the money, they can decide how much to pay doctors. They could control reimbursement amounts to hospitals. They could pass new laws and restrictions on hospitals that increase expenses and thereby increases the public dependency on the HMO's and thereby increase the bureaucracy and move toward socialized medicine. It all sounds like a diabolical Machiavellian plot. It is a slow gradual movement which goes unnoticed in the small steps it takes, but when looked at over a period of time, the ground the government made towards socializing medicine is enormous. The problem is the public doesn't remember life pre HMO, they only know HMO's so they do not realize the successful management of health care prior to HMO's. I think people do realize that HMO's have not been the savior everyone thought they were going to be. How have HMO's adversely affected doctors; well in many ways. You already have seen how they have limited doctor's income, removed the bedside manner from caring for patients, the endless paperwork, the needless fees to join, the wait to receive permission to treat a patient. Many offices have to hire one person just to handle the paperwork. This office person never sees patients, never produces revenue; they are just a hidden cost that has exasperated the increasing cost of medicine. They are an unfortunate yet necessary debit to the payroll.

The problem areas of health care, which have had a negative impact by driving up costs, are Hospitals/Consumers, Lawsuits/Mal Practice premiums, HMO's, Medicare, Medicaid and Prescription Drugs,

Hospitals

In order to manage the post war care, The Hill-Burton law was passed in 1948 providing for 100% financing to hospitals for expansion. Seems like a post WWII provision. Hospitals doubled and tripled in size because as years passed, the number of beds and bed rates became the main determinant in hospital revenues. Returning veterans, economic prosperity, suburban sprawl all contributed to the increase in building new hospitals and the enlargement of existing hospitals. Citizens sort of expected one on every corner which eventually became part of the problem.

As hospital costs increased, due to lawsuits, services and demand, payment became an issue. Insurance companies began to feel the financial strain of paying for health care. No longer could they "toss in" coverage when the client paid for his homeowners. This led the insurance companies into dropping health insurance completely through legislation. As HMO's inherited these expenses, they eventually decided on shortening hospital stays. As HMO's began "practicing" medicine to curtail these costs, patients, hospitals and doctors became more incensed, resulting in the friction in providing health care today.

One other aspect of medical costs is the hospitals themselves. They drive up the costs of medical procedures in the hospitals. For instance, why should a hospital which used to have 300 beds and one hospital administrator now have 90 beds and over 14 administrators, all earning over hundreds of thousands of dollars? Which is more feasible, distributing costs over 300 beds or 90? Which is more practical, charging $500 a night in a 300 bed hospital or $1,000 dollars a night in a 90 bed hospital? Do the math and learn which hospital would earn more. Think about staying another night in a hospital and not worrying about costs. In which hospital would you rather be?

Why does a state the size of CT have 35 hospitals when it could get by with 10? The law stipulates that for a hospital to remain open, it must maintain an emergency room. This sounds okay, but at a cost of $12-15 million, and approaching $20 million a year for each emergency room, that is over a $350 million dollar expense per year just for the emergency rooms. With fewer hospitals, could these savings be spent on more prudent health care needs?

A law in CT was passed 15 years ago stating that any costs for "Hospital ownership" in new machines, i.e. cat scan equipment, could not be disbursed and applied to the bed rate. This forced the hospitals to rent machinery. With 35 hospitals in the state and by law and competition requires a machine in all hospitals, the duplicity and waste becomes enormous. Instead of buying 10 machines for 10 hospitals, 35 hospitals are now renting machines for 35 hospitals, so costs for extra machines are spread over fewer patients and beds, which increase the bed rates. For instance, the bed rate has grown enormously, from a $32 dollar a night stay in the hospital in 1967 to $1,500.00. Patients wonder why a $900 dollar operation ends up costing $10,000. Doctors do too since their fee on average is 14% of the overall costs. Maybe all the money is going to all those overpaid administrators, who do not practice medicine!! If fewer hospitals existed, couldn't savings be spent on more health care issues?!

Doesn't keeping 35 ERs open also strain an already understaffing of nurses and doctors? Isn't there a more practical way of operating the health care in CT? Hospitals are desperate to staff all the nurse's slots. Remember, businesses close at 5 pm, but hospital are open 24/7, 365 days a year. Imagine a business owner with three receptionists for the three eight hour shifts seven days a week. Add these costs onto the bed rates as well. Would more clinics like the one in Essex CT and fewer hospitals save money and provide more staffing at needed hospitals? Most trauma cases get flown to Hartford or New Haven; clinics can manage the simple emergencies, and be located "on every corner" and any serious injuries can be kept alive until an ambulance can reach a hospital and what remains is elective surgery.

Lawsuits

Another factor contributing to the high cost of medical care is lawsuits from all parties. It also contributes to the reasons behind the mass exodus of doctors leaving their profession.

While I am not here to protect the few bad doctors out there, I intend to show how incredibly insane this side of medicine has become. Doctors are in a bind. If they want to remove or de-staff a bad doctor, the doctor in question can sue for constraint of trade. If they must retain the inferior doctor, then the medical staff jeopardizes someone's life. What HMO's have done is create parity, by evening off the dollar amount doctors can charge; people can't identify the good doctors from the bad. How do people usually decide on a good product, a good electrician, or accountant; by price, quality of person and their reputation? Good cars, to good plumbers to good haircuts cost more than bad ones. This way capitalism weeds out the bad doctors. In some sense, wouldn't HMO's policy of parity payment to doctors make it difficult for patients to identify the good from bad doctors?

Some lawsuits initiated by lawyers themselves also have driven up hospital and doctor's costs to illogical levels. How? Think of doctor's mal practice premiums being put into a fishbowl and lawyers swimming around like sharks gobbling up the money.

In the state of Connecticut, lawyers passed a law stating that using restraining methods in nursing home for patients is illegal. Elderly patients sitting in a wheel chair are susceptible to leaning far enough forward to fall out of the chair causing obvious injury. To prevent such disasters, nurses wanted to restrain them to prevent occurrences. Lawyers for whatever reason stipulated this prevention was illegal and passed the law. So, what happened? An unrestrained elderly person did in fact fall and injure herself and the family sued and won. They sued for negligence, "lack of restraint" on patient and won millions of dollars. The nursing home was in a "Damned if you do and damned if you don't bind," could be sued either way. In reality, the lawyers created a law to allow them to sue and make their 33%!!!

A recent piece in the Hartford Courant outlines a comparison concerning payments between doctors and lawyers. This doctor pointed to the fact that the legislative committee researching impeachment of Gov. Rowland retained a lawyer for $500 per hour. The doctor questioned the necessity of this hiring, especially when the federal investigation is underway. The outcome of the investigation will determine if this $500 per hour lawyer is necessary. One does spend money on hiring when it may not be needed.

A woman in CT was awarded $5.2 million dollar in an 11 year lawsuit. According to the article in the Hartford Courant, Sat. Nov. 12, 2005, the doctor examined her and found potential cancer in her breast. Without knowing the full details of the case, the doctor removed her breast. She sued and lost 10 years ago, but won the appeal this week. The doctor saved her life. What if he waited for actual confirmation and it was too late to operate and the cancer spread? He might have been sued for not removing her breast soon enough. The award will be split by the doctor and hospital, contributing to the increasing mal practice premiums. No thanks to the doctor for saving her life. Add this expense to the bed rate to cover future potential lawsuits!! Imagine the expenses the lawyer forced upon the health care profession for ten years....the insurance companies to retain the lawyer, the hospital, any public relations etc! Sorry patient, instead of spending money on you today, we need to settle this ten year case!!

This attitude of searching for any abnormal or untoward outcomes from surgery is mind boggling. Patients are happy to be operated on because if the result is not perfect, it is cause for them to win the lottery. Imagine how the doctor has felt the last ten years with this over his head every time he operates. Will the next hundreds of patients have felt secure, not about his skill, just about his mind going berserk because of this case? Think of a professional athlete being sued by the fans for an error. Think of ballplayers paying a fine for every error committed!! Don't fans experience pain and suffering when their teams lose a big game?

In one of the most famous cases that precipitated the

OB-GYN exodus from practicing is the Florida family who sued a doctor 18 years after the birth of their child. Since the child was not accepted into an Ivy League college, the family concluded that something must have been amiss. When the child's heart skipped a beat during birth, actually leaving the birth canal, oxygen did not make it to the baby's brain for a split second. This lack of oxygen prevented the brain from developing where he could be accepted into an Ivy League college, so the patient sued for mal-practice and won. OB-GYN doctors are now liable for a person's brain development for 18 years, no matter what the person did in that time span; drugs, drinking, or a bump on the head.

One OB-GYN was sued and was approached by the prosecuting attorney to settle out of court. Knowing he had a good case and realizing that the lawyer's first attempt to settle rather than going to court was an admission of a weak case, the doctor did the unthinkable. He did not settle and went to court exposing his name to the public. He eventually won the case but it was a Pyrrhic victory. The Insurance Company spent more money defending the doctor than on a settlement, so they dropped his mal practice coverage. Without coverage, he cannot practice medicine.

Patients can also bring lawsuits. Another example of frivolous lawsuits occurred when a doctor was sued for a rash which developed on a woman's breast caused by a band-aid which remained on for too long. The rash disappeared but the pain and suffering for the rash was too much, so they settled out of court. Don't people have different sensitivity thresholds when it comes to skin?

Another example is the case when a doctor removed the hernia of a female weightlifter. She sued for not repairing the second hernia, which did not show up on the initial X-ray. The second hernia appeared 6 months later after the doctor learned she disobeyed his orders and resumed weightlifting. If you fix a flat in a tire and the tire springs a new leak 6 months later, whose fault is it? The Mechanic, or the driver for driving over the same road?!

The old adage of take two aspirin and call me in the morning no longer applies. Doctors send patients in for too many tests to cover themselves from lawsuits. In many cases the patients may not need all these tests, but the doctor better order them just in case something goes wrong with the patient. If something does in fact go wrong, and a lawyer sees that a certain test was not performed, (probably not needed anyway) the lawsuit begins. This ignites shock in patients when they leave the hospital with a $5,000 dollar bill for several tests and a MRI's for a bump on the head when two aspirin would have been fine. Not an efficient allocation of resources.

Don't believe so? Appearing in a December 19, 2008 article in the Investors Business Daily, it was reported that 9 out of 10 doctors practice defensive medicine, ordering unnecessary tests, referrals they don't need, procedures not warranted etc. This just increases the patient's bill about which they like to complain. So why order the tests? In Mass. 44-48% of doctors reported changing or limiting their practice due to fear of lawsuits. Limiting care and treatment is not conducive to practicing good medicine which inversely has a negative impact on patient care.

Included in the report, 900 doctors found the cost of defensive medicine was $1.4 B in that state alone. Nationally, it is over $210 B. In a New England Journal of Medicine article, reports found that in nearly 40% of malpractice case, no doctor error was committed. Similarly, as many as 80% of all medical litigation verdicts were wrong, unjustified by science. But that did not stop the lawsuits.

Two major mal practice insurance companies are seeking to raise malpractice premiums by as much as 25%. Pro Mutual Group of Boston insures about 3500 physicians and proposes rate hikes by as much as 25%. CT Medical Insurance insures another 2500 doctors in CT. and they propose rate hikes over 14%. If premiums rates are increased 25%, wouldn't that mean that doctor's fees need to be raised 25% just to cover costs. The business practice of passing on expenses to consumers, as corporations do, is impossible in medicine. Do consumers expect doctors to cut costs in medical care to help offset the increase in premiums? As OB-GYN's mal-practice rates increase to over $170,000 dollars per year, is it any wonder these doctors stopped delivering babies?

In an October, 2005 CT State Medical Society Report, the Medicare trustees announced physician payment rates will be cut 26% from 2006-2011, including a 4.4% cut effective on January 1, 2006. The "Concession" doctor's made to Medicare for receiving payment's directly has come home to roost with devastating results. So, as mal practice premiums rise, the doctor's fees decrease, only exacerbating the medical health crisis.

From 1997 to 2000, average awards in mal practice cases almost doubled, from $503,000 to $1 million dollars. Mal practice insurance rates climbed so high, doctors can't afford to pay, forcing them to close their practice and in some cases facilities in which they work. A Las Vegas trauma center did just that, closed its doors because it could not afford mal practice premiums. They did temporarily re open 10 days later when doctors agreed to be "County employees," hardly the employment style they desired. Becoming County employees sounds like government employment and socialized medicine. Next, doctors will be "City employees," then "State employees," and soon after, they will be "Government employees under "Socialized medicine."

Medicare/Medicaid

Title 18 and Title 19, both initiatives under President Johnson's Great Society, has amassed growing and uncontrollable budgets of over $900 billion dollars annually. Title 18 is designed to care for the elderly. Title 19 is to care for the poor. Over 50% of the budget on Medicare is spent on a person's last 6 days of life. Keep them alive so the last child/grandchild can visit. With today's technology and transportation, people will have to make earlier trips to say their goodbyes so these savings can be realized. The patients are being kept alive by machines anyway.

Drug costs

Some citizen groups suggest the US should copy Canada's or Sweden's health care system. They argue how two countries with less GDP than the US can offer universal health care and we can't. Providing universal health care is one of the reasons why they have less GDP than the US. Sweden's tax rate is as high as 70% which is more than twice our highest bracket. Sweden does provide free education through graduate school, but with excessive taxes, what is left over? What about people with no children, or parents who would rather send their children to less expensive schools. How does one balance the financial discrepancies and resolve the arguments between two families where one exploits this opportunity to send their children to the most expensive schools versus the second family is less fortunate and children attend state schools? I don't think that would go over too well here. Besides, too many correlations with Jimmy Carter's presidency and the 70% tax rate in this country didn't work too well. When too much money is drained from investment, productivity suffers, which creates more government dependency, which leads to socialism which is Sweden's government.

Canada's health care system, despite providing universal health care to all its' citizens has serious unmentioned flaws. First of all, every citizen pays a health care bill quarterly. So four times a year, in addition to all their taxes, they pay into their health care system as much as $150.00 dollars whether the person needs the care or not. Secondly, the individual does not select their doctor. The doctor interviews perspective patients and can, depending upon your health, unhealthy habits like excessive drinking, smoking, can decline to accept you as a patient. Consequentially, a patient in need of a doctor might not receive treatment because they were not accepted by a doctor. Doctor's in the US do not close doors on patients. They may not get paid, but they do not deny treatment. My sources in Canada also tell me that getting doctors to return let alone receive phones calls about care are scarce.

They do mention doctors leaving Canada and heading South to the US because conditions are better down here.

Imagine that. Why then do these health care experts suggest universal health care similar to Canada where doctors are leaving for another country?

Consumers/Patients

Patients have become spoiled. When they need a doctor, they usually visit a hospital, even for the most trivial of injuries. Because the population has increased in the last fifty years, the number of these trivial injuries has increased also, which just clogs the ER and burdens the overworked and understaffed nurses. What is the alternative? Is there one?

People also expect a hospital to be on every corner. No longer will people drive more than hour in need of a hospital. They want a hospital nearby. This demanding attitude increased the number of hospitals in Connecticut and in the country, and we know the negative affects this has had on costs and treatments. If the system could change and improve, would the people's attitudes change and improve?

Besides demanding the convenience of having a hospital with all the modern technology next door, they also don't want to pay for it. I personally get tired of watching those movies when the star makes the big stand in the hospital and says, "take care of her Doc, whatever the cost. Whatever the cost!! Just so long as I am not paying for it. When did the attitude develop that health care should be free? I want the plumber here today and I'll pay. I want the electrician here today and I'll pay. I want a doctor here today, but I want it free, just as long as I can afford cable TV!!

The general attitude people have towards doctors and

health care in today's world adds to the costs because of attitudes and expectations. Why do people generally disdain doctors for driving a nice car, or living in a nice house? People today tend to think doctors are charging too much money and that they are the main reason for increases in health care costs. Patients sneer when doctors drive by in a Lexus or Mercedes thinking their hospital stay and the doctor's bill paid for that car.

In contrast, when one examines how citizens treat the businessmen, the professional athlete, and sometimes even worse, the lawyer, the citizens put all of these people on a pedestal. When a lawyer or businessman drives by in their fancy car, people stare in awe and think what a success that man must be. They arrive at this train of thought without even thinking of the prospect that these "successful" people might have fleeced the client or consumer. Lawyers can charge $500 dollars per hour and get away with it, but Doctors can't. How come? Drug companies can overcharge consumers for any product and explain the company needs to be reimbursed for the cost of R & D and marketing for the product over the last ten years. Don't doctors go to medical school for 4 years and train for another 6, so why can't they be reimbursed? It is so ironic to watch people walk in to a hospital and demand the best care money can buy and not have to pay for it. It would be like walking into a car dealer and demanding the best Rolls Royce and having someone else pay for it. These same people who demand the best care without paying for it then spend $500 to $1,000 dollars to go to a sporting event and watch their favorite player go scoreless, hitless, fumble the ball or drop a pass and cause a loss. Instead of paying a doctor for saving their life, they may want to spend "that" money on a flat screen TV! Well, the doctor may want one, so how do they go about getting one? Don't they need to be paid?!!

How can we as rational citizens look at this and not scream? We expect doctors to operate flawlessly, and in most cases they do. It is the extreme and rare cases where operations like amputating the wrong limb happen. It is the untoward outcome that mother nature and the law of averages that make for frivolous lawsuits. Then, these same people who find a minor post operative condition which can be expected or just how the patient reacts, and not be the fault of a doctor, go pay thousands for tickets to watch athletes fail. Why then, can't fans sue the professional for missing a free throw, dropping or fumbling the ball, or striking out or mishandling a ground ball? Aren't they all professionals held to the same criteria as the doctors. How come doctors are paid less and yet expected to be flawless and it is okay for ball players to fail and be paid handsomely for it and not get sued by a season ticket holder.

I know ballplayers defend their salaries by the fact that they have been working towards professional sports their whole life and that they need to make a lot of money because the life expectancy in sports is less than ten years. Well doctors train for ten years before they begin practicing their craft and then when they start, the salaries decrease. How would professional athletes like that? Imagine the league minimum decreasing.

So with HMO's and Obama promising some form of government managed universal health, are they any other solutions. Before solutions, here are some revelations about Universal Health Care.

In an Investors Business Dailey's opinion on Dec. 12, 2008, Charles Krauthammer pointed out as Obama revealed last week: "This painful crisis provides us with an opportunity to transform our economy." Transform is the mission, Crisis provides the opportunity, and the presidency gives him the power. Here is an example of the Government imposing a small step policy, HMO's, to solve the health care problem, "Chaos" (they created in the first place) in the US. When HMO's became pejorative, the people offer the "collective cry" to the Government for help. Its answer is bigger government, or Socialism!!

Regardless of what happens internationally, the big socialistic advancements Obama will promote will be Universal Health Care and some attempt to capture 401K money, or more government control over manufacturing, and housing.

Phyllis Schlafly wrote an opinion in the IBD on Dec 10, 2008 noting the Holyoke Health Center in Boston has patients wait four months just to make an appointment. Massachusetts health plan has been offered as a model for the rest of the US.

Hawaii tried Universal Health Care and disbanded it after 7 months because of its skyrocketing expenses and terrible and timely patient care.

The Mass. Plan forces patients to purchase plans they don't need or want all under the guise to receive the fees to generate enough money to cover everyone....including public funding for abortions.

In a Nov. 11, 2008 piece, the Employee Benefit Research Institute found that 86% of the growth in the total number of the uninsured was due to legal and illegal immigrants. A recent study found only 38% of Americans agree the Government should provide health care, meaning almost two thirds of American, 62%, or a larger percentage of people who voted for Obama DON'T want universal, government run, socialized medicine in America. Universal Health Care, or Socialized Medicine, will be a huge objective for the socialist in Obama's first term. Timing seems right; financial meltdown forces less money to afford, more dependency from higher unemployment, a tribute to the outgoing Ted Kennedy ensuring his legacy, a Hollywood script writer could not come up with a better story.

In a Connecticut Medicine Journal, November 2008, I will quote the author, Melville P. Roberts, M.D. as he summarizes 60 years of Universal health Care under the auspices of the British National Health Service. The BNHS opened in 1948, (post WII Chaos formula to alter life) and within the next year, patient's demands exceeded estimates. Spending increased, problems reoccurred and the patient list awaiting admission reached a high of 1,263,000 in 1998. How long does it take to admit a patient in the states, an hour? A day? The administrative and clerical staff ballooned from 29,021 in 1951 to 280,692 in 2005. Imagine paying for these workers using tax receipts and think if this capital were used actually for providing health care. Didn't I mention earlier that government management of anything grows into an enormous bureaucracy like the HMO's? In the same article, The US enjoys the high cancer survival rate at over 60% while England stands on 44%. If Universal Health care is better, why is this statistic true? Didn't Hawaii just give up state sponsored health care after only seven months? Could Hawaii be used as a test tube example for the rest

of the country and see that socialized medicine is imprac-
tical? Dr. Roberts lastly states that any administration
looking into tax funded health care should look at the
micromanagement, growing costs, compromised treatments and increasing bureaucracy universal health care
fosters as what not to do.

Solution

The solution I recommend encompasses revision in three
major areas of health care: The abolition of HMO's;
decreasing number of hospitals, and revising methods of
providing health care.

Dismantling Health Maintenance Organizations will
address the understaffed, overworked and underpaid
nurses; the under appreciated, under paid, over expensed
over paper worked doctors; the price gouging, controlling
manipulative, financial raping of the public and doctors
by HMO's and lastly to the patients themselves.

HMO's came into existence by filling the void left
by Insurance Companies encouraging laws to be changed
to eliminate health coverage from their policy provisions.
HMO's were a costly experiment that only increased
expenses while simultaneously destroying health care coverage. The government created another huge bureaucratic
middleman and let's face it, for all the costs in operating
an HMO with salaries and wages to workers who don't
even provide one ounce of care is mind-boggling wasteful.
Hospitals used to be run as a non profit health care provider, so why are all these premiums being spent on an
unneeded for profit Wall Street bottom line industry.
Eliminate it.

My idea is to have a personal and private, card carrying

health care accounts with hospitals. Any individual, self-employed, or an employee with or without family can have one. By eliminating HMO's, tax deductible premiums can be mailed to the hospital of choice and deposited into their respective individual account. Tax deductible premiums will be paid until a comfortable balance is reached in which case premium payments cease. This offers numerous benefits for businesses and patients. A dollar limit can be placed on accounts, where payments will have to stop. Obviously, an employee with a family will have higher premiums and a longer payment period to reach the required balance; but that is the employee's choice. If a couple wants to have many kids and can afford them and is willing to pay higher premiums for longer periods, so be it. If a couple just wants a few kids thereby saving money to spend elsewhere, so be it. The choice is the consumer's. This would eliminate the people having too many babies and forcing higher taxes on workers to support them.

For the corporations paying premiums, discontinuing premiums for certain employees who have reached a suitable balance will free up dollars for expansion and more hiring. For the employee, when a balance is reached, individuals can use the increased disposable income for more productive means, savings, investments, purchases. By discussing with their doctor current health care needs and any future health care concerns, individuals can decide how much money in the account is enough. For individual cases where more dollars will be needed, the limit can be increased, but this will be decided by the doctor and patient.

By eliminating the HMO middleman, more premium

dollars will be spent on providing health care, not HMO's expenses. Patients will be allowed to choose hospital and doctor of their choice and to discuss and customize personal health care plan. This eliminates HMO's from interfering and trying to practice medicine, and in causing health care delays for care. Patient and doctor can discuss procedures privately and based on account balance, can decide what is best. They can forgo expensive testing that is applied to insulate doctors and hospitals from potential lawsuits. If an individual or family wants to spend more of their account dollars on extra procedures, or days in the hospital, so be it. It is their money and their health care. Think of it as spending more for options on a car. By allowing the patient to make a health care choice based on price will also help keep health care costs down. For extensive and expensive procedures, a debit non-interest bearing feature will be applied, much like a car loan. Resumption in premiums begins until payment is declared paid in full. If car loans last up to four years, why can't medical payments? For catastrophic care, government assistance can be utilized. This disallows single healthy individuals from being soaked for premium dollars for other people. When individuals realize they may keep more of their pay check, private accounts may act as an incentive for patients to live a healthier life. Discussions about testing, results and procedures will induce an intimate doctor/patient relationship where risks are more easily understood which limits lawsuits. Patients will not have the chance to refute health care decisions and outcomes and look to win the lottery. This method also keeps their medical condition private; it is just between their doctor and them. It removes the possibility of spying of medical folders from curious HMO employees that can be exposed over discussions by the water cooler.

For the family of four with one or both parents working, the method is similar. The company and employee both contribute premiums to this medical account administered at the hospital and not an HMO and the family would receive their respective medical ID cards. Once the family reaches a certain balance comfortable for their needs, the employee can decide to end the contributions. The employee informs the company and both premium payments stop. Any family with more children would obviously have to contribute more. They decided to have more children; it should come out of their pockets. If both parents work, the balance could be reached faster and with fewer premiums dollars from each company, again freeing up more dollars for business expansion.

For payment and records access, a simple ATM like card will suffice. This health care ID card will also store relevant medical records in the hospital for patients which make treating for injuries or health care while traveling easier. For instance an individual from Massachusetts breaks a leg skiing in Aspen. The nurse inserts the card, and medical information pops up on computer screen. All the relevant information is there, blood type, medication, history etc., and contact information of original hospital. Swipe the card and payment is transferred by wire. No paper work, no permission from HMO, no delay etc, just quick and good care.

The abolition of HMO's will free up billions of dollars for health care needs. Concerning Medicare, if one were to install a means of rationing, not as drastic as the one positive component of England's health care policy, additional monies would become available to provide health care. Roughly 50% of Medicare is spent on a person's last six days of life. Add these Medicare savings to the savings from abolishing HMO's, and an annual $1 trillion dollars could be applied to productive health care.

Hospitals

President Johnson asked Dr. Michael Debakey for a solution to the growing health care problem in 1965. Debakey simply said that there are too many hospitals. The solution is to build larger hospitals but have fewer of them. He outlined on a chart of the United States with 25 hospital locations each with a 5,000 bed capacity. There were none in CT. Realistically, the solution is sound, but politically, it is suicide, which is too bad. However, it may come to that if citizens see the wisdom in it.

Consolidating the number of hospitals into large medical centers with increased beds and reassigning the smaller hospitals into other medical needs will save costs and provide efficient care. As Dr. Debakey told President Johnson that the US needs 25 5,000 bed hospitals across the country is accurate. In his chart, CT did not have one hospital. The answer may not have to be this extreme, but a serious look should be taken at this proposal. There are 35 hospitals in CT causing duplicity and excessive waste in dollars. With each hospital mandated to have an Emergency Room at $12 million a year to run and because competition dictates each hospital spends millions of dollars for renting machines, all this is doing is making the GE's rich collecting rent for 35 MRI's when 10 would do, while bankrupting the hospitals ruining health care. If ten hospitals remained open, 25 could close saving at least $300 million just in Emergency Room care. Consolidating hospitals will free money to pay the nurses what they deserve. In some case, they can choose to work less, commiserate with their present salary, also easing the strain on filling nursing vacancies. Fewer hospitals means less in rental expenses, and with larger hospitals with more beds, bed rates will be spread over a larger number of patients, increasing saving. Patients will pay less for lower bed rates.

To use CT in what should take place across the country, I will explain. In reality, CT could survive with fewer larger hospitals located in Stamford, New Haven and Hartford. Recall the difficulty in travel post WWII, no major highways, no helicopters, and lack of means, fewer cars coupled with The Hill Burton Act in the 1940's of 100% financing for expansion in hospitals, spoiled the consumer. Yet in some states, patients will travel hundreds of miles to visit the hospital. Post WWII patients expected a hospital and sometime two in every town. However, improvements in travel and medical technology changed all this. Presently, big city hospitals have more money to spend on technology and equipment so they receive the majority of difficult cases. Helicopters and better roads allow ambulances to make the trip to the big city hospitals and by pass the nearer and smaller hospitals. The medical improvements have allowed them to keep patients alive to make the trip. Medical technology has also allowed the patient to remain at home pre surgery after being diagnosed for an operation. When the time comes to travel to the hospital, will it really matter if the patient travels an hour to the hospital rather than downtown? If explained that savings from closing the downtown hospital will provide for better care and less expense at city hospital, I am sure the patient will make the trip. Shorter stays and out patient surgery means less visits, so the patient doesn't need to be close to the hospital.

With fewer larger hospitals in the big cities, the smaller hospitals can morph into teaching hospitals and clinics. Uninsured patients unable to travel can receive treatment at these teaching hospitals and clinics. Smaller hospitals and clinics can act like satellite offices and hospitals at a fraction of the costs. They can handle minor injuries and surgeries that would only congest emergency rooms at hospitals. Big city hospitals can assign medical residents and interns to these clinics and hospitals and be supervised by area doctors visiting on daily rotations. The uninsured receives treatment while providing experience for the residents at limited costs. Insured people can pay for minor treatment with their ID card, and anything major can be sent to the larger hospital.

For the retired or elderly, they either have an account or they can receive a reduced rate, much like senior citizens receive when paying for movies. Many of the concessions I spoke of earlier are to be applied to the elderly. With fewer hospitals, and more money at the hospitals instead of HMO's, there should be enough money to pay for the expenses. Obviously the neediest should be able to stay in the hospitals. Another concession, with fewer hospitals, I would enlarge the remaining and have included a section for the needy. I would also consolidate and have teaching hospitals mandatory so the future doctors who are on staff can care for the underprivileged. Removing more than 20 hospitals in the state should provide enough staff, interns, and residents to care for the helpless.

Most of their out of pocket expenses for the elderly are for prescription drugs. Hospitals should be allowed to buy in massive quantities for reduced rates directly from the drug companies. The seniors should also receive reduced rates from the hospitals. There is no reason the drug companies should charge that much just to pay the massive salaries and perks. With little to no oversight checking if these profits are being applied to R &D, the opportunity to make obscene profits by the drug companies remains unchecked. Secondly, if the proposed system of having accounts at hospitals were installed, the elderly could receive mail order drugs from their hospitals. Hospitals could debit the accounts and mail them out. No more need for elderly remember to renew subscription, nor trekking out in the bad weather, traveling distances, paying exorbitant prices etc; stay at home a receive your drugs in the mail. Eliminate the CVS middleman for many or all of prescription drug orders. People forget that hospitals are not out to make a profit. When this is true, why should HMO's and drug companies be so concerned to enhance their bottom-line. The HMO's are using the premium dollars to make their profits instead of applying the money where it should go in the first place, to health care.

CONCLUSIONS

According to Norman Thompson, a 1940's US Socialist Party's candidate for president: "The American people will never knowingly adopt socialism, but under the name of liberalism, they will adopt every fragment until one day, America will be a socialist nation." "Every "fragment" means any government sponsored policy will initiate control over the populace and foster government dependency and further the "nanny" state.

As I have shown in this book, the four major areas of our society have been transformed from a free market society to one of Government support, i.e. Socialism. The Globalists have used whatever means to create the Chaos which necessitates Government control. You have read how these areas, Banking, Trade, Taxes, and Health care worked prior to The Globalists manipulations, witnessed the transformation from free market to socialism aka a "nanny state" and have learned their perpetuation schemes.

Establishment of these organizations breaks down the sovereignty of nations. Unelected officials overrule our elected officials in the management of our country. The Globalist have accomplished the accumulation of power, be it government through the United Nations, and money, through the Federal Reserve, and through the WTO with Trade, and through some new unnamed Health Care Provider for Health Care, to transfer control over each from the millions of citizens to the few

Globalists. They strengthen their purpose with excessive and progressive taxes to perpetuate their causes. They make conditions dire enough to have citizens moan their "Collective Cry" for government assistance as presently being used for Health Care! This is creating the "chaos" to promote socialized medicine.

Has someone else witnessed and predicted these coming events? None other than one of the smartest men in the twentieth century, one with the second highest Grade Point Average (behind Robert E. Lee) in the history at West Point, General Douglass MacArthur. In his thoughts and opinions from "Revitalizing a Nation" revelations from his duration as magistrate in post war Japan, MacArthur mentions several thoughts that while they seemed obscure when written in the 1950's, are certainly more obvious in today's world.

He writes that there are those who wish to destroy the sanctity of our, the US, religious base, to abolish private property and free enterprise in order to secure the degree of power over material things necessary to render absolute power to suppress the spiritual things. A socialistic government first establishes collectivism, a hiding place for those who lack self reliance, or for those who like government dependency. This is a half way step towards Communism. Once private control over means of production is lost to the government, human freedom will eventually be suppressed. The result is a nanny state and socialism.

MacArthur further states that this threat is not external, but internal. These forces which aim to alter our society have infiltrated journalism, education, and the media, all to manipulate the masses by perverting the truth, impair respect for moral values, suppressing human freedom and destroying the faith in religious teachings.

MacArthur quotes Thomas Jefferson in stating the greatest danger is public debt, and leaders who load the economy with debt risk our independence, our liberty and any continuing of expanding on debt will arm the Magistrate with patronage that will be used to corrupt the government. Is anyone thinking of lobbyists? How about the creation of government jobs to curry favors during prosperous times which are unsustainable in economic downturns?

There are those who are constantly trying to alter our concept of freedom and human rights. There are those who plan to alter the constitutional checks and balances of government established to preserve the integrity of our branches of government. There are those who seek to make the burden of taxes so great and the progressive increase so alarming, that the nation will end up inert and stultified; thereby becoming servants to the state. There are those that want the Government to assume Oligarchic powers; to reshape or discard the moral and ethical principles which built this great nation, into socialist and narrow political purposes to serve their goals. The Globalist's agenda is outlined in this book. We, as citizens, cannot allow the government to engage in behavior modification, instructing us how to live, eat, what to drive, where to live etc.

MacArthur warns that progressive taxation and the sharing of wealth to protect not only the US but other countries would reduce our standard of living to the level of universal mediocrity. I used the seesaw example. We cannot allow for the establishment of an egalitarian society where conspicuous consumption is reserved to the few who make the rules. Citizens also cannot allow this same group to enact laws which they ignore, but force the populace to obey. I referred to the two tier class society.

Under the stress or "Chaos" of two national emergencies, and two world wars, there has been a persistent and progressive power grab by the Federal Government with little or no restoration of those rights back to the individual states once the crisis subsided. Authority specifically reserved to the states has been ignored in the effort to centralize power with the Federal Government. It reminds me of the "Chaos" formula.

Where once our economy thrived under free enterprise, the shift has occurred through confiscatory taxation towards a socialistic state and country. Need I say more?

The remaining tax potential is so depleted, (think of number of types of taxes) that any future emergencies or obligations will result in the direct confiscation of capital, or the printing of new money!! Attempts to take 401k money, auto maker's bailouts and TARP money come to mind. This is the blueprint to Socialism, and the question facing our people is should we preserve freedom or yield to the formula of centralized government under the concept of Socialism?

The Socialistic perpetrators use the paternal instinct of the Federal Government to produce a progressive weakening of the structure of the individual character. Therefore, the sovereign communities and states will be transformed into the subservient states under the federal direction in direct proportion to the dependence upon federal grants for local support. Excessive taxation enables this paternal direction and saps the remaining workforce from taking risks and seeking the initiative inherent in fostering a free market, capitalistic and prosperous society. If this continues, no nation can survive if the people become servants to the state. Currently, The Federal Government of the United States and State Government in CT, employ more people than there are manufacturing jobs. Where did the middle class go? This means a shrinking private sector tax base is being forced through progressive and excessive taxation to support the growing number of public employees.

Wow, how prescient? If this has not happened where are you hiding your head?!! By allowing all this to happen under the guise of progressiveness, globalism, or liberalism (and not combating these viewpoints), is exactly how we got to where we are.

FINAL THOUGHTS

Incarceration Expenses

The prison expenses, both caring and providing for the prisoners and the salaries and wages for the men who guard them, have become for many states and the federal government a significant portion of the budget. Is there a better way of managing this program while getting something beneficial from the prisoners for the general welfare and simultaneously ensuring a safe community while cutting expenses? The answer is yes.

Why not separate prisoners into two categories, one hard core 10 to life, and the second under 10 years.

With Group 1, Hard Core, 10 to life, I would remove them totally from society and reinstate a form of penal colony. No longer will taxpayer's money be used for three meals, a bed, a roof, cable TV and conjugal visits. We can't make incarceration better than life outside of it for the prisoners.

We certainly have an island in the Pacific leftover from WWII where minimal housing, tents, and Quonset huts could be erected. If these arrangements were good enough for our soldiers who fought to keep our country free, then it should be good enough for prisoners.

Collect the criminals, and transport them to this establishment where escape is futile. Food, shelter, beach all provided, even sunscreen! Monitor prisoners with a GPS bracelet, and keep watch with surveillance cameras, a Navy or Coast Guard ship. Any prisoner who serves his/her sentence could be retrieved. This would make it difficult for prisoners to escape and endanger society with a home invasion, armed robbery etc. This element is totally removed from society.

With a large number of Group One gone to the Pacific, more space will become available for the minor offenders thereby eliminating early parole because the prisons are too full. While some will remain in prison, some can be rehabilitated and some we can use in the workforce. The "safe" ones (if there are any in that group) can be shipped to the farm areas to "Do the work no one wants," as cited by the liberals who enjoy "Illegal Immigrants" performing those tasks. Why not have a man sentenced for a year, (certain Governors and Wall Street executives fit the bill) be sent to farms to grow food for free? Why can't welfare recipients harvest food? They would be less likely to foul the harvest with disease like the illegals have done, if they knew the food would be eaten by US citizens. Why not have minimum-security prisons be set up to be self sustaining? Why not have these prisoners work for contractors and landscapers where the minimum wage is paid. They can receive the wages upon completion of sentence. Can one imagine Ken Lay from Enron, or Dennis Kozlowski, or the culprits from the recent credit crisis cleaning the NYC streets, planting flowers on Park Ave. Public humiliation is a wonderful deterrence for second offenses. Potential first time offenders observing public figures performing menial tasks is also a strong message.

Which brings me to the Illegal Immigrant issue? I am for "LEGAL" immigrants at a yearly rate suitable to the country's ability to absorb them into society without burdening the taxpayer. I am against "ILLEGAL IMMI-GRANTS" but am pro-assimilation, and want English spoken and no Spanish on my ATM or public buses. Try walking into a class at any college (They are mostly all Liberal) and take a course without filling out an application. One would be kicked out immediately. How hypocritical for a professor to remove a student from class who has not been accepted into the college, but accepts illegal immigrants into their country without a proper application.

Costs of Illegal Immigration are enormous. $11 to $22 Billion is spent on welfare for illegal aliens each year. Over $2 Billion is spent on both free school lunches and Medicaid for illegal aliens. $17 Billion is spent on educating "Anchor Babies" the American born children of illegal immigrants. In addition to the sex crimes committed, remittances, (wages earned in US but monies returned to families in Mexico) and other statistics, the final tally is over $338 Billion dollars a year spent on illegal immigrants. Add the $700 Billion dollars we send overseas buying oil from tyrants, Chavez and Putin, instead of drilling in the US, totals to over a $1 Trillion dollars mismanaged by our Government. Is this on purpose to "merge the US and Soviet Russia fostering a One World Order of Socialism? One can verify these statistics at Homeland Security at tinyurl.com/t9sht and at transcripts.cnn.com.

According to Laura Ingraham, in "Shut Up and Sing," California spends $3 billion dollars of taxpayer money a year to subsidize the illegal immigrants, albeit this figure includes, besides emergency medical care, education and social services. That is still a large number especially when asking the taxpayer to subsidize "ILLEGAL" immigrants.

I don't mind the legal immigrants, heck my forefathers were legal immigrants. They eventually worked hard and learned the customs and became citizens and eventually I was born a citizen entitled to these provisions and rights just as I would consent to the same care for a "LEGAL" immigrant. It is the "ILLEGAL" immigrants or a non US citizen I don't want to subsidize. Why does the US provide comparable care to "ILLEGAL" immigrants as they do for US citizens when so much more can be done to care for our citizens and "LEGAL immigrants? When looking at $3 billion for California, what do you think this figure is when one adds all the expenses for all ILLEGAL immigrants in all fifty states? Florida, estimate $3 billion? NY, another $3 billion?! Add it all up and I am sure it is a significant amount. The total is over $330 billion dollars every year the US spends on illegal immigrants, health care, education, housing, food etc.

Let's just say the estimate is $333 billion dollars spent subsidizing ILLEGAL immigrants each year. That same $330 billion could either be used to provide health care for the "US citizens" or "LEGAL immigrants or could have been removed from the taxes collected, or could have been spent on , Health, Education, Veterans Affairs, etc. Imagine all these illegal immigrants getting subsidized by your fellow hard working taxpayer.

A US Census Bureau estimate reveals a net increase of 500,000 illegal immigrants will reach the US each year. The problem only worsens unless something is done.

When the US was more of an industrial and manufacturing country, the county could absorb the legal immigrants but with these manufacturing jobs fleeing the country, and legal immigrants arriving, how does this country and taxpaying citizens afford this additional burden of an ever increasing number of "ILLEGAL" immigrants? The Government just passes the expense on to the taxpayer.

While presently this country seems to be on a downslide, now is the time for America to hark back to the days of their forefathers, the generations who made this country what it became. We, as a country need to look ourselves in the mirror and ask what is best for the US. Is it better to return the manufacturing jobs back from China and promote domestic employment or keep the jobs in China? Is it better to increase the tax base by doing so, or devise new and higher taxes on the decreasing number of workers? Is it better to lower taxes so people can buy products labeled with "Made in the USA" tags knowing this purchase might help their neighbor who made it instead of some unknown worker in China? Yes! By doing this, would this worker receive wages to become self reliant and remove themselves from a nanny state government dependency program? Yes!

Once the jobs we used to perform return, reestablishing the middle class, all else will fall into place. Increased employment, increased tax base, increased tax revenues, increased self reliance, decreased government dependency, will improve society, the standard of living and general welfare, decreased crime, fostering a return of a once prominent productive society.

As I am submitting this book to my publisher, the fore-closure/banking Wall Street meltdown is occurring. This is a final example (until the next one) of the Globalists coercion to create "Chaos" using the monetary and fiscal institutions to alter life in the United States and steer it towards a one world socialistic government. In brief, back in 1977, Jimmy Carter signed into law the Community Reinvestment Act. This Act was designed to curtail "redlining," the practice of having banks move into downtrodden neighbors, accepting bank deposits and loaning money to out of town citizens. This Act encouraged banks to loan to the poorer communities without regard to the borrowers' ability to pay. Sounds like redistribution of wealth!

President Clinton encouraged even further that banks lend money to borrowers despite the fact the borrowers used welfare checks as collateral. Some lending institutions even provided "NINJA" loans, or No Income, No Job, and No Assets and as little as a 5% down payment to borrowers all in the name of fulfilling the American Dream to people who could not afford it.

The changes in banking and mortgage origination contributed to the meltdown as well, but more of a symptom not the cause. In the past, a loan officer in a bank received a salary and loaned money from deposits in their banks, their own money in other words. They were more diligent in reviewing loan applications and were not influenced by price, just affordability. Now, when banks and mortgage brokers "find" money, they can inflate the price of the house because they earn a commission on the loan. Secondly, since the money is not in their bank, they don't care about due diligence, the three year tax returns, a 20% down payment, the phone call to the employer; they just find the money to loan and keep a commission.

Big Wall St institutions seeking to make huge profits

bought these mortgage backed securities not realizing how many were overleveraged. When mortgage payments included both interest AND principle and the adjustable rate mortgage increased, and the economy softened, you have a perfect storm financial crisis. People have less money to pay the higher mortgage, (one they never should have received) and banks did not receive these payments and the crisis snowballs.

So how does this fit in to invoking socialism? The CRA allowed for public release of lending evaluations and performance ratings of banks boosting pressure from public groups like ACORN to bully banks into making more "NINJA" loans. Despite many warnings from everyone, Congressmen, Greenspan and Treasury Secretaries, and attempted legislative reforms brought by Republicans, Barney Frank, Ted Kennedy, and Chris Dodd, (the Chairman of the Banking Committee) all refused reform and said things were fine. Federal Reserve Chairman Tim Geithner and Senator Dodd also has attended these Globalists/Bilderberger meetings which will play out later.

The Head of Fannie Mae from 1999-2005, Franklin Raines overstated the profits so he could award himself over $100 million in severance upon his departure. He did allow Countrywide to give Chris Dodd a favorable loan, while doling out Fannie Mae contributions to Dodd, Obama and Franks, all three of whom received over $120,000 dollars in campaign contributions. Franklin went on to become Obama's Chief Economist during his campaign. To add insult, Clinton's Treasury Secretary Robert Rubin received over $100 million in severance from Citibank when he resigned in 2005. What is it about the year 2005 that has these two heads of major banking and real estate companies leave at the same time, taking a hefty paycheck to boot. Coincidence?

This "Chaos" plays into the Globalist hands in two ways. Remember when President Bush wanted to privatize Social Security, but the Democrats denied that prospect. They denied it because they didn't want to lose taxpayer's money to spend on their causes, and secondly, they did not want individualism, the everyday citizen becoming more self reliant and less dependent on them, the government. Remember what I said in Taxes, they, the Socialists, want to tell the workers how long to work, and how much to pay in taxes. Current suggestions now include the government taking over the housing, the banking, and even the workers 401K money. Imagine receiving one check for your social security and 401K money realizing a weak return of 3% annually. They create the fear to have people run to the government to save them. In return the citizens will accept concessions, where to live, where to bank, how to live and potentially to accept the government to manage their retirement funds. If the government had trouble with Government run operations like Fannie, does it make sense to allow them to manage our investments? Now who does one presume Obama will have to solve this crisis? Rubin, Volker, etc are arriving onto the scene on a White Horse as saviors, heck they started this. This is the perpetuation I mentioned, the so called experts, who after creating the mess, offer suggestions with socialistic concessions.

BIBLIOGRAPHY

William J. Gill, *Trade Wars Against America*. Praeger, (Westport, CT. 1990)

Ron Chernow, *Alexander Hamilton*, (The Penguin Press, New York, 2004)

Ron Chernow, *The House of Morgan*, (Touchstone, Simon & Schuster, NY 1990)

Ron Chernow, *The Warburgs*, (Vintage Books, Random House, NY. 1993)

Laura Ingraham. *Shut Up & Sing*, (Regnery Publishing Inc. 2003)

Niall Ferguson, *Empire*, (Penguin Books, 2004)

Douglas MacArthur, *Revitalizing a Nation*, (The Heritage Foundation, Chicago 1952)

Alan P. Jones, *How The World Really Works*, ABJ Press, (Paradise CA.1996)

William T. Still, *New World Order*, (Huntington House, 1990)

FOOTNOTES

1. William J. Gill, *Trade Wars Against America*. Praeger, (Westport, CT. 1990) p.55
2. Ron Chernow, *The Warburgs*, (Vintage Books, Random House, NY. 1993) p.4
3. Ibid. p. 10
4. William T. Still, *New World Order* (Huntington House, 1990) p.143
5. Alan P. Jones, *How The World Really Works*, ABJ Press, (Paradise CA.1996) p.106
6. Niall Ferguson, *Empire*, (Penguin Books, 2004) p. 15
7. Niall Ferguson, *Empire*, (Penguin Books, 2004) p. 19
8. Niall Ferguson, *Empire*, (Penguin Books, 2004) p. 29
9. Niall Ferguson, *Empire*, (Penguin Books, 2004) p. 226
10. Ron Chernow, *Alexander Hamilton*, (The Penguin Press, New York, 2004) p.110
11. William T. Still, *New World Order*, (Huntington House, 1990) p.148
12. Ibid. p.147
13. Wall Street Journal Guide to Investing.
14. Niall Ferguson, *Empire*, (Penguin Books, 2004) p. 186
15. Ibid. p. 190
16. William T. Still, *New World Order*, (Huntington House, 1990) p.152
17. Niall Ferguson, *Empire*, (Penguin Books, 2004) p. 190

18. William T. Still, *New World Order₂* (Huntington House, 1990) p. 159
19. Ibid. p. 153
20. Ibid. p. 153
21. Ibid. p. 149
22. Ron Chernow, *TheHouse of Morgan,* (Simon & Schuster, NY 1990) p.123
23. William J. Gill, *Trade Wars Against America.* Praeger, (Westport, CT. 1990) p.59
24. William T. Still, *New World Order₂* (Huntington House, 1990) p. 147
25. William J. Gill, *Trade Wars Against America.* Praeger, (Westport, CT. 1990) p.63
26. Alan P. Jones, *How The World Really Works*, ABJ Press, (Paradise CA.1996) p.109
27. William J. Gill, *Trade Wars Against America* Praeger, (Westport, CT. 1990) p. 94
28. Almanac, The Hartford Courant
29. William T. Still, *New World Order₂* (Huntington House, 1990) p. 174
30. Alan P. Jones, *How The World Really Works*, ABJ Press, (Paradise CA.1996) p.57
31. William J. Gill, *Trade Wars Against America.* Praeger, (Westport, CT. 1990) p. 145
32. Ibid. p. 169
33. Ibid. p. 13
34. Ibid. p. 17
35. Ibid. p. 39
36. Ibid. p. 48
37. Ibid. p. 75
38. Ibid. p. 120
39. Ibid. p. 222

40. Ibid. p. 46
41. Ibid. p. 46
42. Ibid. p. 55
43. Ibid. p. 123
44. Investors Business Daily, Sept. 21, 2001
45. Hartford Courant, Feb. 15, 2004
47. Ibid
48. William T. Still, *New World Order*, (Huntington House, 1990) p. 154

CPSIA information can be obtained at www.ICGtesting.com
Printed in the USA
267273BV00005B/3/P